PROOF IT!

▶ A Competency-Based Approach to Proofreading and Editing Skills

▷ by
George S. Amsbary

South-Western Publishing Co.

Editorial
Executive Editor: Carol Lynne Ruhl
Acquisitions Editor: Randy Sims
Developmental Editor: Marilyn Hornsby
Coordinating Editor: Angela McDonald
Consulting Editor: Judith S. Voiers

Production
Production Manager: Deborah M. Luebbe
Senior Production Editor: Jane Congdon
Associate Editor: Dawn M. Goodman

Art and Photography
Designer: George McLean
Art Coordinator: Barbara Libby
Associate Director/Photography: Diana Fleming (cover photo)

Marketing
Marketing Manager: Colleen Thomas

Quality Assurance (Software)
Senior Quality Assurance Specialist: Michael Jackson

Copyright © 1994

by SOUTH-WESTERN PUBLISHING CO.
Cincinnati, Ohio

ALL RIGHTS RESERVED

The text of this publication, or any part thereof, may not be reproduced or transmitted in any form or by any means, electronic or mechanical, including photocopying, recording, storage in an information retrieval system, or otherwise, without the prior written permission of the publisher.

Library of Congress Cataloging-in-Publication Data

Amsbary, George S.
  Proof it! : a competency-based approach to proofreading and editing skills / by George S. Amsbary
     p. cm.
  ISBN 0-538-70944-8
  1. Proofreading. 2. Editing. I. Title.
Z254.A47 1994
686.2'255--dc20   93-18927
                                                                CIP

1 2 3 4 5 6 H 98 97 96 95 94 93

Printed in the United States of America

Contents

Preface   vii
Introduction to Proofreading   xi

Lesson 1
Proofreader's Marks and Spelling   1

The Proofreader's Marks   2

    Delete Sign, Close Up Space Sign, Insert Sign   2
    Insert Punctuation Signs, Insert a Period Sign   3
    Replace or Substitute Sign   4
    Transpose Sign, Move Within Text Sign   5
    Move Outside Text Sign, Center Sign, Align Sign   6
    Add Space Sign   7
    Hyphen Sign, Begin New Paragraph Sign, No New Paragraph Sign   8
    Leave As Was Signs ("stet")   9
    Spell Out Sign, Make Boldface Signs   10
    Make Italics Signs, Make Lowercase Signs   11
    Make Lowercase into Capital Signs   12
    Insert Parentheses Sign, Insert Dash Sign, Keyboard Spacing Signs, Query the Author Sign   13
    What Else? What If There's Not Enough Room?   14

The I-E Spelling Rule   17

Lesson 2
Proofreading for Basics, Subject-Verb Agreement, Subjects vs. Objects, Spelling   19

The Sentence—Some Basics   21
Subject-Verb Agreement   23

    With Nouns   24
    With Compound Subjects   24
    With Pronouns   25
    With Irregular Verbs   25
    With Indefinite Pronouns   26
    With Fractional Subjects   27
    With Separation in Space   27
    Wrap-up   28

Subjects vs. Objects   30

    Nouns as Objects   31
    Pronouns as Objects   31

Three Kinds of Objects *32*

    Direct Objects *32*
    Objects of Prepositions *32*
    Indirect Objects *33*

The Final Silent E Spelling Rule *35*

Lesson 3
Proofreading for Commas, Semicolons, Spelling   *37*

Punctuation I *38*
Commas — What Do They Do? *38*

    The Four Uses of Commas *39*

Semicolons — What Do They Do? *46*

    The Semicolon as a Balancer *46*
    Words That Signal Semicolon *47*
    The Semicolon as Super-Comma *47*

The Final Y Spelling Rule *50*
The Change for Plural Spelling Rules *51*

Lesson 4
Proofreading for Periods, Question Marks, Exclamation Points, Parentheses, Dashes, Brackets, Colons, Spelling   *53*

Punctuation II *54*
Periods — What Do They Do? *54*

    Short Sentences *55*

Questions and Exclamations *55*

    The Question Mark *56*
    The Exclamation Point *56*
    Some Other Uses of ? and ! *56*

Parentheses, Dashes, and Brackets — The Fences *60*

    Parentheses *60*
    Dashes *60*
    Brackets *61*

Colons — The Announcers *63*

    Other uses of the Colon *63*

The Double Consonant Spelling Rule *66*

Lesson 5
Proofreading for Apostrophes, Quotations, Asterisks, Ellipses, Hyphens, Slashes, Spelling   69

Punctuation III   *70*
Apostrophes — What Do They Do?   *70*

    Apostrophes Show Possession   *70*
    Apostrophes Can Show Omission   *72*

Quotation Marks — What Do They Do?   *74*

    Enclosing Direct Quotations   *74*
    Enclosing Words That Define a Noun   *74*
    Enclosing Exact Thoughts   *75*
    Enclosing Certain Titles   *75*
    The "Sub-Quote" or "Single Quote"   *76*
    Special Rules for Multi-Paragraph Quotations   *76*

Asterisks and Ellipses   *78*
Hyphens — How To Use Them   *81*

    End-of-Line Hyphens   *81*
    Words That Must Be Hyphenated   *82*

Slashes (Virgules) — What Do They Do?   *85*
The Final CE/GE Spelling Rule, The Final OE Spelling Rule, and DIS/MIS/UN/AS/IL/IR Prefix Rules   *87*

Lesson 6
Editing: Wordiness, Redundancy, Outdated or Overused Expressions, Cliches, Precision, Logic   89

Editing   *90*
An Editor's Questions   *90*

    Is It Accurate?   *90*
    Is It Clear?   *93*
    Is It Logical?   *94*
    Is It Concise?   *95*

Avoid the Passive Voice   *98*
Wrap-up   *100*

Correct Markings for the "Let's Try" Exercises   101

Official State Abbreviations   115

Preface

Introduction

Proofreading is becoming increasingly important as business communication becomes increasingly fast. Fast and frequent communication carried at the speed of light by FAX, phone, and photo simply means more and more communication—and more and more chance for error. Errors in communication can cost businesses money—sometimes millions, sometimes even billions. That's why more and more employers look for people who have training or experience in proofreading. Today, most everyone must proofread once in a while.

What Proofreading Really Is

Proofreading is the process of catching mechanical and content errors in something someone has written, typed, or keyed onto a screen or a piece of paper, and correcting those errors by making certain generally agreed-upon signs or marks.

Proof It! Improves Your Proofreading

Catching and correcting errors—this is the basic information taught in *Proof It!*. Learning to catch and correct errors (i.e., learning to proofread) is easier than learning to write without making any errors. So in *Proof It!* the emphasis is on providing the clues to help you discover errors easily and to help you find the easiest way to correct them. As a student you can become a competent proofreader, whether or not you're a good writer. You have been speaking, writing, hearing, and using the English language for a couple of decades or more by now, and you have a good sense of what looks or sounds right, whether you know why it's right or not. So *Proof It!* simply reminds you of the basic grammar you've already had, and then challenges you with many proofreading jobs, trial exercises, group exercises, and tips on how to catch and correct errors.

FEATURES

- **You Learn To Make the Proofreader's Marks First** You can't proofread on paper until you know how to mark the errors you find. In Lesson 1 of *Proof It!* all the commonly used proofreader's marks are illustrated and defined, and frequent opportunities for you to practice drawing them clearly are provided. Moreover, the first two specific objectives to be achieved for *Proof It!* are to draw correctly and identify 33 proofreader's marks.

- **You Learn Where the Most Frequent Errors Are** The most frequent errors you will encounter as a proofreader are errors of subject-verb agreement, misuse of personal and possessive pronouns, excessive or inadequate punctuation (especially commas, semicolons, apostrophes, and hyphens), and misspellings. *Proof It!* presents easy techniques for finding and recognizing such errors, including spelling rules which will enable you to spot misspellings of most of the common words you'll ever encounter.

- **You Learn the Grammar Related to Proofreading** The traditional grammar terms that you will deal with most are limited to *noun, pronoun, subject, object, verb, clause, singular, plural, past,* and *present.* These are defined in easy-to-understand terms, supplemented with entertaining explanations, examples, training diskettes, overhead transparencies, and plenty of practice exercises.

- **You Learn by Doing Actual Proofreading Jobs**

1. *"Let's Try" Exercises:* Beginning in Lesson 1, as you learn the proofreader's marks, you will find after the description and illustration of every few marks a feature called "Let's Try." This gives you a trial run at proofreading using the marks you have just learned. Each of the six lessons contains several "Let's Try" exercises at strategic points, giving you a chance to practice actual proofreading.

2. *The Template Diskette:* You may practice these same "Let's Try" exercises, as well as Class Exercises provided in an easy-to-use template diskette. Usable in IBM® and IBM®-compatible computers, the diskette will give you invaluable practice at making corrections related to what you are learning in the *Proof It!* text directly on screen.

3. *The Class Exercises:* Each lesson in *Proof It!* contains one or more "Class Exercises." These give you a chance to practice proofreading either with the rest of the class in group session, with a classmate, or by yourself as homework.

4. *The Overhead Projector Transparencies:* You get another chance to exercise the proofreading skills you are developing by contributing to a full-class proofing of a Class Exercise or an alternate passage either by calling out the correction needed or by actually making the correction with the proper mark on the transparency.

5. *The Job Sheets:* The 30 Job Sheets, available from the instructor according to his or her directions when you feel you are ready to do them, are the means by which you prove your competency.

IBM is a registered trademark of International Business Machines Corporation.

They are actual jobs to do to a certain standard of correctness. Some request that you demonstrate your knowledge (such as how to make each proofreader's mark, or which of the given pronouns are always subjects, which are always objects, and which could be either). Others are stories or documents containing errors to be proofread. When you successfully perform the job described in each Job Sheet, you will have achieved the specific objective to which the Job Sheet relates. Job Sheet performance determines the grade you will get, as your instructor will explain.

- **You Learn in a Competency-based, Individualized System**
Educators have discovered that the opportunity for students to learn (especially in skill-learning) is greatly enhanced in a competency-based, individualized learning system. The core of a competency-based, individualized system (and, therefore, of the *Proof It!* text) is made up of precisely stated behavioral or performance objectives. *Proof It!* contains 30 such objectives, each beginning with a strong active verb (such as *Draw, Match, Name, Identify, . . .*), followed by what specifically is to be done, what is given, and the performance standard to which the task must be accomplished. The Job Sheet, when done to the standard defined by the objective, becomes the achievement of the objective.

All the information in the *Proof It!* text and ancillary media (template disks, instructor clarification, overhead transparencies, etc.) is that which is needed to achieve the objectives. The instructor is primarily a manager, enabling students to achieve as many of the objectives as possible within the time constraints of the course. Assessment of student competency is accomplished simply by counting the number of Jobs successfully done (i.e., the number of specific objectives achieved) and relating the number to whatever grading standard your institution has adopted. The burden of learning is on the student; the burden of managing the system, and enabling and encouraging the student to learn is on the instructor.

Instructor's Guide

Day-by-day materials needed and suggested techniques for presentation, group activities, individual activities, and points to emphasize are provided in the *Instructor's Guide* for the *Proof It!* text. Keys to the Class Exercises in the text; photocopy masters of each of the Job Sheets, in addition to the Keys to each Job Sheet; transparency masters; and the template diskettes are included. Also included is a reference section that can be used to prepare transparencies or can be copied and provided to students. The *Instructor's Guide* is carefully organized so that even relatively inexperienced new or substitute instructors can handle a class on any given day.

Message to Students

You can be sure you will learn from this text. This *Proof It!* text was developed by an author who knows well the problems of proofreading from the top administrative and editorial positions he has held with leading encyclopedia and educational publishers and the U.S. Government. He has his advanced degree in English from Harvard, and has written and/or acted as prime editor of hundreds of curriculum manuals in a score of different subject matters. He currently teaches a broad age-range of students in a private career school the applications of communication theory to micro-computer operation.

This competency-based, individualized *Proof It!* program has undergone nearly two years of testing with nearly 1,000 students in a post-secondary, private, ACCET-accredited business school utilizing 12 instructors of widely differing backgrounds in English (ranging from instructors holding advanced degrees in English from Harvard to those with advanced engineering or accounting backgrounds). Only rarely did a student have to redo particular Job Sheets more than three or four times before achieving the related objective. Students expressed delight that they had the chance to rectify their errors, instead of being "stuck with a lousy grade." The tenor of their reaction to the system was, "I was glad finally to get a chance to really learn things."

You, too, will learn from *Proof It!* And because *Proof It!* uses an informal, conversational tone for all examples, instructions, and exercises, you will enjoy using this text as you build your proofreading skill.

Conclusion

The author and the publishers are proud to make available to teachers and students this competency-based, individualized basic course devoted specifically to learning the skill of proofreading. When students who have learned from the *Proof It!* text take their places in the rapidly moving, electronic world of business, communication will be considerably clearer and more accurate.

George S. Amsbary

Introduction to Proofreading

The whole idea of proofreading is to find and correct errors. Sometimes you will proofread directly from the computer screen. When you do that, you can make your corrections directly. All you have to do is push a button to Delete, Insert, Replace letters, spaces, words, or other groups of characters.

But sometimes you have to find and correct errors on a piece of paper—a printout, a typed letter, a scribbled note from the boss, etc. You can't make your corrections directly, then. You have to make some marks to show how you want the errors corrected.

Of course, the marks you make must have some meaning to the person who is going to make the corrections (and that might be you!). That's why a collection of proofreader's marks that are understood throughout the English-speaking world have been developed. And these are the proofreader's marks you will be learning.

Two Kinds of Errors

When people write, type, or key words, they make one or both of two kinds of errors—*mechanical* and *content*.

Good proofreaders usually read through the text twice. Sometimes two people do the proofreading. One holds the copy and reads it aloud while the other marks all the corrections to be made. They trade off holding and marking to keep from becoming tired and careless. But most of the time, one person has to do it all by himself or herself. The first reading is to find *content* errors.

Does the copy make sense? Is the sequence of sentences logical? Is the grammatical structure correct?

The second reading is to find *mechanical* errors (and many people find mechanical errors best by scanning lines backwards).

Are the capital letters correct? Is all the punctuation okay? Spacing?

Be a Nitpicker

Proofreaders read very carefully. For example, the proofreaders in a well-known national magazine are required to place a dot under every letter and space in the text they read and mark every error, no matter how small. Then they must initial the copy they have proofread. Later, if an error is found in the finally printed copy, the proofreader of that copy is fired if one dot is missing.

A proofreader must really concentrate and have sharp eyes. He or she must assume that errors *do* exist, must know basic grammar, and must know how to spell correctly. Above all, he or she must know the proofreader's marks.

All the lessons in this book will give you the practice you need to become the sharp-eyed, nitpicking proofreader you should be. Also, you'll learn some spelling rules that will help you catch most of the spelling errors you'll come across.

The Proofreading Job Sheets in This Course

At the beginning of each lesson in this book is a list of learning objectives. For example, you see that Objective Number 1 is: "Draw correctly, with 100% accuracy, 33 different proofreader's marks that are most commonly used throughout the English-speaking world." Job Sheet 1 gives you the opportunity to do just that and, thus, prove that you achieved Objective Number 1. If you do Job Sheet 1 (in this case) 100% accurately, you get an OK; if you are not 100% accurate, you must study your errors, get a clean Job Sheet 1, and redo it. Your instructor will have the appropriate Job Sheets available. You may redo each Job as many times as necessary to accomplish it successfully.

The whole course contains 30 performance Objectives for you to achieve, and each has a related Job Sheet for you to do to prove that you have achieved the Objective. Twenty of the Objectives are basic. Achievement of these basic Objectives (to the performance standard described in the statement of the Objective) indicates a basic and minimally acceptable mastery of proofreading skill. Ten additional Objectives (marked with an asterisk [*] following their numbers) are available. Achievement of all ten (to standard, of course, and in addition to the basic twenty) indicates maximal mastery of job-entry level proofreading skill.

You are expected to achieve at least all Objectives without asterisks. It is suggested, therefore, that you do those first during the time allotted for each Lesson (usually a week or so). If you have time, of course, you are encouraged to try also to achieve the Objectives marked with asterisks so you can attain the highest job-entry level proofreading skill you can. School officials will describe more specifically how your Job accomplishment record will relate to your training record.

Now, let's learn how to *Proof It!*

Lesson 1

Proofreader's Marks and Spelling

When you complete this Lesson, you will be able to achieve the following objectives:

Objective Number 1: Draw correctly, with 100 percent accuracy, 33 different proofreader's marks that are most commonly used throughout the English-speaking world.

Objective Number 2: Identify, with 100 percent accuracy, the kind of error for which each proofreader's mark is to be used, given appropriate definitions and examples.

Objective Number 3: Spell correctly 16 out of 20 words that follow the I-E Spelling Rule, when these words are pronounced orally.

Objective Number 4: Spell correctly 8 out of 10 words that are exceptions to the I-E Spelling Rule, when these words are pronounced orally.

The Proofreader's Marks

The following pages contain the marks or signs used by virtually all proofreaders. Each is named and illustrated, along with a description of how the mark is used. Notice that the illustrations are drawn freely, naturally; that's the way you should make them. When you mark an error, do it quickly; don't labor over your drawing. At the same time, do it clearly. You want the person who is going to re-key what you've proofread to make the changes accurately.

DELETE Sign

Used to delete single characters, words, numerals, or groups of words.

Examples: developement   We want to thank you.
development   We thank you.

I got a $5,000,000 check from my uncle.
I got a $5 check from my uncle.

CLOSE UP SPACE Sign

Used to show where blank space within text should be closed up.

Example: What you say can not be true.
What you say cannot be true.

NOTE: Most proofreaders use the close up space sign along with the delete sign if they are deleting a character or characters within a word. The combination shows that an open space is not to be left where the deletion takes place. See the following:

Deletions create space.
Deletions create space.

INSERT Sign

Used to show where an insertion of a space, character, numeral, word or words is to take place. It can show insertion from below (∧), above (∨), or sides (> or <).

Examples: convient   In God Trust   It is not to say.

convenient In God We Trust It is not for me to say.

2

INSERT PUNCTUATION Signs

Used to insert punctuation marks in text. These are the insert sign (∧) plus the various punctuation marks that are to be inserted. Some punctuation marks are inserted from below and appear "under the tent," whereas others appear from above—"in the basket."

INSERT COMMA **INSERT SEMICOLON** **INSERT COLON**

INSERT QUESTION MARK **INSERT EXCLAMATION**

INSERT APOSTROPHE **INSERT QUOTATION MARKS**

Examples: "Thank you, she said.
"Thank you," she said.
Why didnt you tell me?
Why didn't you tell me?
Learn a lot earn a lot.
Learn a lot; earn a lot.
He was a tall dark and handsome man.
He was a tall, dark, and handsome man.

Martha s Vineyard
Martha's Vineyard
Hurray, we won
Hurray, we won!
At 10 22 p.m.
At 10:22 p.m.

INSERT A PERIOD Sign

Used to show where a missing period should be placed. It is a period with a circle around it, and it does not require the insert sign (∧).

Example: Mr and Mrs Jones attended
Mr. and Mrs. Jones attended.

▶ LET'S TRY! 1-1

Mark deletions, insertions, and close-ups in the following sentences.

0. You should always make your proofreader's marks quickly but clearly.

1. The the goal of business is to make a proffit.

2. Sucessfull busines people know that they cann make more profit in the log run if they sell a quality product and if theyy have go od publick relatins.

3. A customer [insert apostrophe] s good will de pens upon how much and wat kind of service he or she gets.

4. Goodwill also depends upon wheather business executives apear to have the [insert quotation marks] You Attitude [insert comma] " rather than to bee thinking of themselves or their business alll the time.

5. So it is correct to saye that in busiess one can do well by doing goode.

(Check your work in the Correct Markings section at the back of this book.)

(TEMPLATE USERS: Complete this exercise using your template disk.)

REPLACE or SUBSTITUTE Sign

Used to replace or substitute letters, words, or numbers. This sign is a line crossing out letters, numbers, or words that are to be replaced with different letters, numbers, or words. No delete sign or insert sign is needed when new letters, numbers, or words are substituted for original ones—just the cross-out line and the new letters, numbers, or words.

Examples: ~~yesterday~~ today   elig~~a~~ible
today   eligible
We received ~~no~~ ̭otes. seven
We received seven votes.

TRANSPOSE Sign

Used to transpose letters, numerals, or groups of words. The curves of this sign's sideways "S" shape may go either way.

Examples: adn   1949   the for moment
and   1994   for the moment

MOVE WITHIN TEXT Sign

Used to move a word, numeral, or group of words or numerals from one place in the body of text to another.

Circle the part to be moved and draw an arrow to where it is to be inserted.

Examples: He only could count on one friend.
He could count on only one friend.

He is a member; he is not an outsider.
He is not a member; he is an outsider.

After all, it was spring. He wanted to take the day off.
He wanted to take the day off. After all, it was spring.

$17.43 was what Petra owed.
Petra owed $17.43.

▶ LET'S TRY!   1-2

Mark replacements, transpositions, and moves within text.

0. Yes, just the spendthrift sutdent had enough money for a taxi.

1. There are at leest seven days in a work weak.

2. Teh beat qualifciation you have can to get a job is pedendability.

3. What shoudl I say? "He could count on one only friend," or "He only could count on one freind."

4. I can listen to you the for moment, but nit for awl day.

5. The way to write one thousand in numreals is 10,00.

(Check your work in the **Correct Markings** *section at the back of this book.)*

💾 (TEMPLATE USERS: Complete this exercise using your template disk.)

5

MOVE OUTSIDE TEXT Signs

Used if you want to move lines or blocks of copy to the right, left, upward, or downward. The *closed end* of the bracket shows the *direction* of the move (e.g., ⟶).

Examples:

MOVE RIGHT ⟶ Now] is the time to go.

MOVE LEFT ⟶ [Now is the time to go.

MOVE UP

MOVE DOWN ⟶ [Now is the time to go. / Now is the time to go.]

CENTER Sign

Used to show what should be centered. Two reversed brackets show that titles or headings should be centered horizontally on a page.

Example:

]CENTER THIS HEADING[
        CENTER THIS HEADING

ALIGN Sign

Used to show where and how text should be aligned. Two vertical lines show that lines of text should be aligned at either the right or left margin.

Example:

‖Now is the time   Now is the time
  for all good men   for all good men
    to come to the aid   to come to the aid
  of their party.   of their party.

LET'S TRY!   1-3

Correct the following passage by centering the title and adjusting the spacing and alignment.

```
       ⃝]WRITTEN REPORTS[

      ⌐When⌐I am given an assignment that requires a
    ‖written report, I first prepare a list of steps
            that will help me to complete the report by
                the due date.

   ]FORMATTING A REPORT[

   There are probably dozens of correct ways to format a
   short written report, but the way I learned works well for
   me.  First, I center the main heading at the top of the page,
   using all capital letters.  Then I leave a space blank and
   start the text.  It's pretty standard, I think, to start each
         new paragraph indented five spaces from the left margin.
      After that, of course, all the lines go back to the left

   margin until the end of the paragraph.
         If you're using a subheading within the report, you should
   set it off in some way, probably by putting it on a line by
   itself.  I usually underline it or, if I can, use italic or
   boldface type.
```

(Check your work in the **Correct Markings** *section at the back of this book.)*

   📀 (TEMPLATE USERS: Complete this exercise using your template disk.)

ADD SPACE Sign

     Used to indicate when additional space is needed within text and looks like a "pounds" sign. It is most often used with the insert sign.

Example:
```
         It is time#for class to#begin.
                  ^           ^
         It is time for class to begin.
```

7

HYPHEN Sign

Used with the insert sign to show where a missing hyphen should be placed. It looks like an equal sign with two horizontal lines so that it will not be confused with the dash or other proofreader's marks.

Example:

> This is state∧of∧the∧art equipment.
> This is state-of-the-art equipment.

BEGIN NEW PARAGRAPH Sign

Used to show where to begin a new paragraph. Note that the sign looks something like a backward letter "P" with a second line drawn in.

Example:

A paragraph may be quite short. ¶ A sentence, which is a group of words containing at least a subject and verb and expressing a complete thought, may be quite long, on the other hand.

    A paragraph may be quite short.

    A sentence, which is a group of words containing at least a subject and a verb and expressing a complete thought, may be quite long, on the other hand.

NO NEW PARAGRAPH Sign

Used to close up separated paragraphs. Write "no" in front of the backwards "P."

Example:

    A paragraph may be quite short.
no ¶ A sentence, on the other hand, which is a group of words containing at least a . . .

    A paragraph may be quite short. A sentence, on the other hand, which is a group of words containing at least a . . .

Let's Try! 1-4

Mark correctly the addition of spaces and hyphens, and indication of paragraphing.

0. "I'm not perfect," he said. "But you just know that everybody is a whole lot better off under my management than they were before. Let me tell you why. First, we did not choose run-of-the-mill equipment. Instead, we . . ."

   It's no fun working with old fashioned computers. All computers cannot be the most current, of course. Still, it would be good if all offices and all schools could have the pleasure of having state-of-the-art computers. [Mark a new paragraph here] Ironically, it is the computer industry itself that keeps us from getting truly state-of-the-art computers. You see, they come up with new ideas so fast that, by the time we get the latest thing they develop, they have already developed something else that is truly more powerful, and what we have is no longer state-of-the-art equipment. [Do not begin a new paragraph here] It isn't fair, is it?

(Check your work in the Correct Markings section at the back of this book.)

(TEMPLATE USERS: Complete this exercise using your template disk.)

LEAVE AS WAS Signs ("stet")

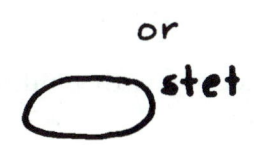

Used when you want to undo proofreader's marks you or someone else made previously, either because the marks are in error, or you decide the indicated change should not have been made.

Printers call this "stet." Either place dots under what you want to "leave as was," or encircle it and write "stet" by the circle.

Examples:

occasionally   or   occasionally stet
occasionally   occasionally

SPELL OUT Sign

Used when it is necessary to spell out abbreviations or numerals rather than to leave them in their abbreviated or numeric form. Circle what you want to have spelled out, and write "sp" next to the encirclement.

Examples: Oct.   4   600
                Exec. Secy.
                October four   six hundred
                Executive Secretary

▶ **LET'S TRY!**   1-5

Mark "stet" (leave as was) and spell out situations.

0. The Corp. office hours are not always convenient.

1. Sometimes even proofreaders make mistakes, and if a sec'y happens to catch a proofreader's mistake, he or she should become a super proofreader and mark it "stet."

2. The principal officers of the company are Natalie Jones, Chair of the Board; Juan Gonzales, CEO; Yashima Ogata, Pres.; and Lu Wong, Treasurer.

3. A person should always count ~~his or her~~ *their* change before leaving the cash reg.

(*Check your work in the* **Correct Markings** *section at the back of this book.*)

🖫 (TEMPLATE USERS: Complete this exercise using your template disk.)

MAKE BOLDFACE Signs

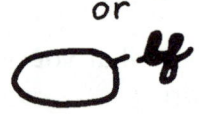

Used to emphasize characters, words, or passages with boldface print.

Examples: DANGER   or   DANGER
                DANGER   **DANGER**

(*NOTE:* Don't use both alternatives at the same time.)

10

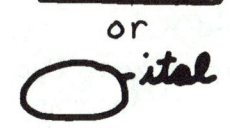

MAKE ITALICS Signs

Used to indicate that the following should be printed in italics *(letters that slant the way these do)*:

- Book, movie, and play titles;
- Foreign phrases;
- Names of newspapers, magazines, and artistic works;
- Characters, words, or passages of text to be emphasized.

An underline in typed or handwritten copy becomes italic *(italic)* when set in type or keyed on a computer typesetting machine. The people who do typesetting know that the underline is the proofreader's mark for *italics*.

Examples: Sophie's Choice becomes *Sophie's Choice*
The New York Times becomes The New York *Times*

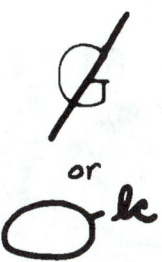

MAKE LOWERCASE Signs

Used when capital letters should be lowercase letters. With just one or two letters to change, use the first mark shown — a simple slash through the letter. If whole sentences or phrases must be lowercased, encircle what you want to change, and write "lc" next to the circle.

Examples: Gone With The Wind becomes *Gone with the Wind*
We PICKED them becomes We picked them

NOTE: Book or movie titles are generally written in caps and lowercase, which means that the *initial* letters of all words but *articles*, *conjunctions*, and *prepositions* are capitalized. If a title appears in all caps (such as GONE WITH THE WIND) and you want to make it caps and lowercase, encircle it and write "clc" next to the circle.

Example:

GONE WITH THE WIND becomes *Gone with the Wind*

11

MAKE LOWERCASE INTO CAPITAL Signs

Used when lowercase letters should be capitalized. Use three horizontal lines under the letters that should be CAPS if there are only a few. For longer passages to be changed, draw a circle around the words and write "cap" or "caps" next to the circle.

Examples:
```
Will nasa ever get the shuttle up?
Will NASA ever get the shuttle up?
Will nasa ever get the shuttle up?
Will NASA ever get the shuttle up?
```

Let's Try! 1-6

Mark boldface, italics, capitals, and lowercases.

0. Here's how to mark: Boldface or Boldface, Italics or Italics, capitals or capitals, LOWERCASE or LOWERCASE, caps and lowercase.

Some people think that to emphasize words or phrases it is appropriate to use boldface type, which you show in this way: **Spring is here!** or Spring is here! But others disagree. They think you should use italics, which you show in this way: *Spring is here!* or Spring is here! Still others think you should emphasize by using all capitals, which you show in this way: Spring is here! or Spring is here!

Nobody, though, would show emphasis by making a capitalized word or phrase all lowercase, but if they wanted to change all caps to all lowercase for some other reason, they would show it in this way: SPRING IS HERE! or SPRING IS HERE! And if they wanted to make it caps and lowercase as it would appear in a title, they would show it this way: spring is here and everywhere!

(Check your work in the Correct Markings *section at the back of this book.)*

(TEMPLATE USERS: Complete this exercise using your template disk.)

INSERT PARENTHESES Sign

Used to insert parentheses. Draw a parenthesis (whichever one needs to be inserted), make two hashmarks across it to prevent it from being confused with any other markings. Put an insert sign below it at the point where it is to be inserted.

Example: (I think I'm right .⧸ (I think I'm right.)

INSERT DASH Sign

Used to insert a dash. Draw a dash (as long as two hyphens on a typewriter), make two hashmarks across it (again to prevent it from being confused with some accidental mark), and put an insert sign below it at the point where it is to be inserted.

Example:

Here I come ready or not.   Here I come — ready or not.

KEYBOARD SPACING Signs

Used to indicate how many vertical line spaces to make on a typewriter or computer keyboard.

Examples:

To say "make single-spaced" on keyed copy:	>SS
To say "make double-spaced" on keyed copy:	>DS
To say "make triple-spaced" on keyed copy:	>TS
To say "make quadruple-spaced" on keyed copy:	>QS

QUERY THE AUTHOR Sign

Used to question the author. If something doesn't make sense to you in the document you are proofreading, and you can't figure out how to correct it, you must ask the person who wrote it: "What do you mean?" To do that, draw a circle around the questionable part and write a big question mark by the circle. Don't put in an insert sign (∧), or someone may think you want to insert a question mark.

Example: Blue is different from green, (odm'y oy).?

Blue is different from green, **[plus whatever the author changes** *odm'y oy* **to – probably** *isn't it*.**]**

13

What Else?

It is possible that you may have to make some proofreader's marks that haven't been shown in the preceding pages. Chances are they'll be inserts; you may have to insert a bracket, slash, asterisk, or ellipsis. Put an insert caret (∧) at the point where such punctuation should be inserted, and put the punctuation above it.

⌐ ⌐ / ∧ ∧	INSERT BRACKET
/ ∧	INSERT SLASH
✻ ∧	INSERT ASTERISK
⋯ ∧	INSERT ELLIPSIS

What If There's Not Enough Room?

If the print is small and the lines are close together, it's difficult to make proofreader's marks right on the line. Look at the passage below to see how to solve that problem:

Example:

By en rolling in this school you are showing that you realize you're living in the neew Age of Communications. You are part of the Knowledge and Information Revolutoin. You understand that the important jobs in this day and age are the ones that have to do with spreading knowlege and information in shout, with communicatfing. You've made a good decision.

14

▶ LET'S TRY!   1-7

Mark insertions of parentheses, dashes, brackets, slashes, asterisks, and ellipses.

0. Brackets look like this: [ ]; the slash looks like this: / ; the asterisk looks like this: * ; and ellipsis dots look like this: ... .

　　Reading proof [insert left parenthesis] i.e., the "proof" that what was meant to be typed on a keyboard actually was typed and printed out [insert right parenthesis] demands concentration [insert dash] not relaxation and enjoyment and [insert ellipsis] well, you know what I mean.

　　Proofreading is finding and correcting errors.[insert asterisk] Concentration is required because (even though the original copy may be very neat [and neatness is important[insert right bracket] [insert right parenthesis] an error could possibly appear with each character you look at.

　　A good proofreader seems to enjoy the concentration [insert dash] even when he or she proofreads his or her own writings [insert left parenthesis] that is, when he or she is a combination writer [insert slash] proofreader).

*An error is a faulty use or non-use of the proper forms of words and sentences, misuse of punctuation, or misspelling.

(Check your work in the **Correct Markings** *section at the back of this book.)*

　(TEMPLATE USERS: Complete this exercise using your template disk.)

Class Exercise 1-1

Directions: There are errors to be corrected with proofreader's marks in the following passage. You may team up with a classmate, if you wish, to find and mark them correctly.

GIGO

The underlying problem in communication is the difficulty people have saying what they mean. Human beings make mistakes once in a while. They mispell words, they put commas where they don't belong, and don't put commas where they do belong, they use the wrong word, they get into a hurry and don't finish sentences, and so on. In fact, human beings make mistakes quite frequently.

Get rid of the Garbage

Mistakes aren't so bad if they get corected. But computers are not going to correct them. Oh, there are programs that will beep or groan when you inadvertently key in a misspelled word (provided that word is in the computer's dictoinary), but you are the one who must correct the speling, if youre doing the keyeing. But computers will still print out garbage if you (or someone else) put garbage into them. GIGO ("Garbage In; garbage Out) still accuratly describes how computers work.

The point is that this wonderful Age of Communication, this Knowledge Revolution, in which you live, is going to make the (not) world any better if it produces garbage. It (not will) succeed, and niether will you succeed. You must be the one who keeps the garbage from getting into the computer (or the printing press, the air waves, or the sound and picture on the TV screen). And if the garbage is allready there, you must be the one to get it out.

(TEMPLATE USERS: Complete this exercise using your template disk.)

JOB READY? You should be ready to do Job Sheets 1 and 2 now!

The I-E Spelling Rule

You probably have heard or learned this version of the I-E Spelling Rule:

*It's "i" before "e," except after "c,"
Or when sounded like "ay" as in "neighbor" or "weigh."*

But that rhyme has many exceptions. For example, look at the words in this crazy sentence:

Neither species of *weird financier* will *seize leisure either.*

There's another rhyme to help you remember the I-E Rule. It seems to have fewer exceptions:

*When the vowel is sounded like "bee,"
Then the "i" comes in front of the "e."
But it's "e" before "i" if the pair of them follow a "c,"
Or if they're sounded like "ay" as in "neighbor" or "weigh."*

Here are some words that are spelled with "ie" that rhyme with "bee," and DON'T immediately follow a "c":

believe, achieve, yield, thief, chief, fiend, niece, piece, relieve, shriek

And here are some words that are spelled with "ei" that rhyme with "bee," and DO immediately follow a "c":

receive, deceive, conceive, conceit, ceiling, deceit, receipt, perceive

And here are some words in which the "ei" is sounded like "ay":

neighbor, weigh, weight, freight, vein, seine, reins

ALL THESE WORDS FOLLOW THE RULE. But we still have the exceptions:

*neither, either, species, weird, financier,
seize, leisure, height, forfeit, ancient, their*

You just have to learn them. Look in the dictionary for others.

17

▶ **LET'S TRY!** 1-8

Find and correct with proper proofreader's marks the words that disobey the I-E Spelling Rule. (As an example, the first line is correctly marked.)

He received the reciept and felt that he acheived the goal he had always beleived in. Happily, he put the receipt in his breifcase and began walking to the feista where he was supposed to meet his neice. No longer would she greive over the loss of her office and her place in the heirarchy of the club. Now she would be releived, not of her position as cheif, but in her heart. She would get a repreive. And he could take a seista while he waited for her to arrive.

(Check your work in the **Correct Markings** section at the back of this book.)

(TEMPLATE USERS: Complete this exercise using your template disk.)

JOB READY? You should be ready to do Job Sheets 3 and 4 now!

Didn't you read *Proof It!*? It's *oxen* before *person* except after *cart*.

Lesson 2

Proofreading for Basics, Subject-Verb Agreement, Subjects vs. Objects, Spelling

When you complete this Lesson, you will be able to achieve the following objectives:

▶ **Objective Number 5:** Match with 100 percent accuracy the terms *noun, pronoun, verb, subject, object, singular, plural, masculine, feminine, neuter, past, present, future, collective nouns, clause,* and *sentence* to their definitions.

▶ **Objective Number 6*:** Proofread, using the correct proofreader's marks, the faulty subject-verb agreements in simple, compound, and complex sentences. Performance standard: 90 percent accuracy.

▶ **Objective Number 7:** Proofread, using the correct proofreader's marks, simple, compound, and complex sentences containing faulty subject-verb agreement so that the subjects and verbs of the sentences agree. Performance standard: 100 percent accuracy.

▶ **Objective Number 8*:** Proofread, using the correct proofreader's marks, sentences containing errors in subject-verb agreement. Performance standard: 100 percent accuracy.

▶ **Objective Number 9:** Proofread, using the correct proofreader's marks, a list of sentences containing errors in the use of indefinite pronouns, fractional subjects, separated subjects and verbs, and exceptional kinds of nouns. Performance standard: 100 percent accuracy.

▶ ***Objective Number 10*:**   Identify with 100 percent accuracy from a given list of pronouns those which are in the form of objects by marking them with the letter "O"; those which are in the form of subjects by marking them with the letter "S"; and those which are in a form that may be either an object or subject by marking them with the letters "SO."

▶ ***Objective Number 11:***   Proofread, using the correct proofreader's marks, sentences containing errors in objective or subjective forms of pronouns, subject-verb agreement, and spelling so that those forms are correctly used. Performance standard: 100 percent accuracy.

▶ ***Objective Number 12:***   Spell correctly 80 percent of an orally given list of words that follow and are exceptions to the Final Silent E Spelling Rule.

The Sentence — Some Basics

To be able to proofread or edit what you or other people write, you have to know how a basic sentence is put together. You don't have to have a Ph.D. in grammar and syntax, but you **do** have to know a few of the words and ideas that experts in grammar use when they talk about *the sentence*.

1. **Be able to recognize which words are *nouns, pronouns,* and *verbs* in a sentence.**

    A **NOUN** is a name (or a word used) that means a **person, place, thing,** or **idea**. For example, the following words can be nouns:

`Mary   John   woman   man`	(These are person nouns.)
`forest   city   Albuquerque`	(These are place nouns.)
`automobile   computer   paper`	(These are thing nouns.)
`democracy   love   hatred   reason`	(These are idea nouns.)

    A **PRONOUN** takes the place of a certain noun in a sentence, usually the noun that goes before it.

`The car hit Anne, and she was injured.`	("She" is the pronoun that takes the place of "Anne.")
`The boat, which was painted red, sank.`	("Which" is the pronoun that takes the place of "boat.")

    A **VERB** is a word or a group of words that *tells the action or state* of a noun, or *links* a noun with another part of the sentence.

`The storm ruined the house.`	(The word "ruined" is the verb. It shows the action of "storm" on "house.")
`That man is a tennis player.`	(The word "is" is the verb. It links the nouns "man" and "player.")

2. **Be able to recognize which words are *subjects* and which words are *objects* in a sentence.**

    A **SUBJECT** is the noun or pronoun in a sentence that **performs the action** that the verb describes.

`The dog bit the jogger.`	(The subject, "dog," performed the biting.)

    An **OBJECT** is the noun or pronoun in a sentence that **receives the result of the action** that the verb describes.

`The dog bit the jogger.`	(The object, "jogger," received the bite.)

3. **Be able to recognize which words are *singular* and which are *plural*.**

   The student [SINGULAR NOUN] studies [SINGULAR VERB] hard.

   The students [PLURAL NOUN] study [PLURAL VERB] hard.

   The media [PLURAL NOUN] are asking [PLURAL VERB] hard questions [PLURAL NOUN].

4. **Be able to recognize *compound* subjects, objects, and verbs.**

   When sentences have two or more subjects, objects, or verbs, they are called compound subjects, objects, or verbs.

   Ian, Billy, and Jean [COMPOUND SUBJECT] played and won [COMPOUND VERB].

   The ball hit the tree, the window, and the couch [COMPOUND OBJECT].

5. **Be able to recognize *collective* nouns.**

   Some nouns mean more than one person, place, thing, or idea, but are still used as singular nouns. *Group, staff, company, committee* are examples.

6. **Be able to recognize whether a group of words is a sentence or not, and to recognize clauses within sentences.**

   A **CLAUSE** is really a sentence within a sentence, and always contains a subject and a verb, understood or expressed. A clause either acts independently or is dependent upon the rest of the full sentence to complete the thought.

   I went to the store, and I bought a shirt. [TWO INDEPENDENT CLAUSES]

   When I went to the store [DEPENDENT CLAUSE], I bought a shirt [INDEPENDENT CLAUSE].

   A **SENTENCE** is a group of words with a subject and a verb that expresses a complete thought.

   When I went to the store. [NOT A SENTENCE; IT EXPRESSES AN INCOMPLETE THOUGHT.]

   I bought a shirt. [A GOOD SENTENCE; IT HAS A SUBJECT AND A VERB AND EXPRESSES A COMPLETE THOUGHT.]

   If you can recognize these parts and know what these terms mean, you'll be able to be an excellent proofreader and save your company a lot of mistakes.

Let's Try! 2-1

Recall the names of words or groups of words by the ways they function in an English sentence.

Directions: In the blanks write the correct name of the term that is described. One of the following words should be written in each blank: *noun, pronoun, verb, subject, object, clause.*

clause 0. What is a sentence within a sentence?

noun 1. What is the name of (or word used for) a person, place, thing, or idea?

subject 2. What is a word that *performs* the action that an action verb describes?

verb 3. What links subjects with objects or descriptions of subjects?

pronoun 4. What is a word that substitutes for a noun?

object 5. What is a word that *receives* the action described by an action verb?

verb 6. What is a word (or group of words) that tells the action a subject is performing?

verb 7. What is a word (or group of words) that tells the state of being of a subject, or links a subject to another part of a sentence?

Clause 8. What is a group of words that has both a subject and verb, and acts either independently in a sentence (as a sentence within a sentence), or is dependent upon the rest of the sentence to complete the thought of a sentence?

(Check your work in the Correct Markings *section at the back of this book.)*

(TEMPLATE USERS: Complete this exercise using your template disk.)

JOB READY? You should be ready to do Job Sheet 5 now!

Subject-Verb Agreement

Subjects and verbs must agree with one another. That means a *singular subject* must be the subject of a *singular verb*; a *plural subject* must be the subject of a *plural verb*.

With Nouns

When the subject is a noun, all you have to know is whether the subject is singular or plural. *Singular* means *just one*; *plural* means *more than one*.

Examples:

singular subject/singular verb
The large lake **steamer/carries** many passengers.

plural subject/plural verb
Large lake **steamers/carry** many passengers.

> ▶ **A PROOFREADING TIP** ◀
>
> Singular nouns usually DO NOT end in "s"; singular verbs usually DO end in "s." Plural nouns usually DO end in "s"; plural verbs usually DO NOT end in "s."

With Compound Subjects

Compound Subjects Joined by "and" Take a Plural Verb

Some sentences have two or more singular subjects. For example, "Sarah *and* Bob take the ski lift." *Sarah* is a singular subject and *Bob* is a singular subject, but these singular subjects are joined by "and." Just as 1 + 1 = 2, Sarah + Bob = two (meaning more than one, or *plural*). Therefore, the total subject is plural and must have a plural verb. "Take" is the plural form of the verb; it does not end in "s."

Compound Subjects Joined by "or" or "nor" Take a Singular Verb

A similar sentence that has two or more singular subjects is, "Sarah *or* Bob takes the ski lift; the other walks." This time notice that the verb "takes" is in its singular form. Why? Because this time the subjects are joined by "or" and the sentence says only one of the two subjects takes the ski lift. This sentence even says "the other walks." If only one subject, no matter how many subjects the sentence has, *performs the action described by the verb*, then the verb must be in its singular form.

> ▶ **A PROOFREADING TIP** ◀
>
> Some compound subjects, such as *pepper and salt* or *the red, white, and blue* are considered as one thing (singular), so they take a singular verb even though they are joined by "and." (Have you ever asked for the salt at the dinner table, and had both the salt and pepper passed to you?)

With Pronouns

The way most nouns change from singular to plural is in the addition of the letter *s* at the end, but PERSONAL PRONOUNS change in different ways. Look at the following list of the singular and plural forms of personal pronouns.

Singular Personal Pronouns	Their Plural Forms
I	We
You	You
He	They
She	They
It	They

All the personal pronouns in that list can be subjects of sentences. For examples, *I take the ski lift; you [SINGULAR] take the ski lift; he takes the ski lift; she takes the ski lift; it takes the ski lift; we take the ski lift; you [PLURAL] take the ski lift; they take the ski lift.*

The subjects and verbs in all those sentences agree. **But look at the form of the verb that goes with "I" and the singular "you."** It's "take," and "take" doesn't have the *s* on the end; "take" is the plural form of the verb, but the subject is singular. All the rest of the personal pronouns go with verbs that are of the same form as they are when they go with nouns – the singular form of the verb has an *s* at the end, and the plural form of the verb does not have an *s* at the end. **But the singular subject personal pronouns, "I" and "you," take the plural form of a regular verb.** All you can do is remember this situation. Actually, it is not difficult. You've been speaking and writing English for many years now, and chances are you would never say: "I take*s* the ski lift" or "You take*s* the ski lift." It just doesn't sound right.

With Irregular Verbs

Most verbs are regular. That is, they keep the same form (WITH the *s* at the end) when they are singular, and they keep the same form (WITHOUT the *s* at the end) when they are plural, and when they refer to the past (with *ed* or *en* at the end).

But verbs that relate to "being," "having," "doing," or "going," are irregular. They change form depending upon whether the action takes place in the past or the present, and whether the subject is singular or plural. Also, if the subject is a personal pronoun, the verb changes form depending upon whether the subject is "I" or "we" (1st person), the singular "you" or the plural "you" (2d person), or "he," "she," "it," or "they" (3d person). In other words, irregular verbs change form a lot, and you just have to know the different forms. Again, it should be easy, because you've been using the language for a long time, and you're used to these changes. Wrong forms don't sound right or look right.

As a reminder of how these irregular verbs change form with personal pronouns, see Table 2-1 — Irregular Verbs. Notice how the verbs change form, but also notice that there aren't many changes. The changes are just different from the usual change with regular verbs — the simple adding of the letter "s" for the singular form of the verb, and leaving off the "s" for the plural form of the verb. If you read aloud while you proofread, you'll probably know when someone has made a mistake in these form changes, because it won't sound right.

JOB READY? You should be ready to do Job Sheets 6* and 7 now!

With Indefinite Pronouns

Many pronouns are indefinite. They don't refer to a specific person, place, thing, or idea. Some of these indefinite pronouns are always singular, some are always plural, and some can be either singular or plural, depending upon the meaning of the sentence.

TABLE 2–1   Irregular Verbs

"Being" Verbs	"Having" Verbs	"Doing" Verbs	"Going" Verbs
Present Singular	***Present Singular***	***Present Singular***	***Present Singular***
I am	I have	I do	I go
You are	You have	You do	You go
He is	He has	He does	He goes
She is	She has	She does	She goes
It is	It has	It does	It goes
Past Singular	***Past Singular***	***Past Singular***	***Past Singular***
I was	I had	I did	I went
You were	You had	You did	You went
He was	He had	He did	He went
She was	She had	She did	She went
It was	It had	It did	It went
Present Plural	***Present Plural***	***Present Plural***	***Present Plural***
We are	We have	We do	We go
You are	You have	You do	You go
They are	They have	They do	They go
Past Plural	***Past Plural***	***Past Plural***	***Past Plural***
We were	We had	We did	We went
You were	You had	You did	You went
They were	They had	They did	They went

The Always-Singular Indefinite Pronouns — *another, any one, anybody, anyone, anything, each, either, every, every one, everybody, everyone, everything, neither, no one, nobody, nothing, one, some one, somebody, someone, something.*

Examples:

Every student *has* problems. *Each needs* help of some kind. *One has* to be patient. *Everyone is going* to the graduation ceremony. *Something tells* me it will be exciting.

The Always-Plural Indefinite Pronouns — *both, few, many, others, several.*

Examples:

Several students *were* furious, but *others were* happy. *Many are* called, but *few are* chosen.

The Either-Singular-or-Plural Indefinite Pronouns — *all, any, more, most, none, some.*

Examples:

All the pudding *is* eaten. ("Pudding" is singular.)
BUT *All* the grapes *are* eaten. ("Grapes" is plural.)

With Fractional Subjects

A **fractional subject** is a subject that is in the form of a fraction, such as *one-half, three-quarters*, and *fifteen-sixteenths*. Remember that the way to make the fractional subject agree with the verb (or make the verb agree with it) is to figure out whether the fraction is a single part of one thing. If it is a single part of one thing, it's obviously singular. But if the fraction refers to a number of things, then it's plural and takes a plural verb.

Examples:

The car wasn't totaled, but *three-fourths* of it *was* damaged.
(There was one car; three-fourths of it is a singular concept.)

Two-thirds of the people *dislike* where they live.
(There are many people; *two-thirds* of them are still many, and therefore plural.)

With Separation in Space

Sometimes the subject of a long sentence is separated from the verb by a long distance. As a proofreader, you have to be alert to what the subject is, and not forget it. Be sure the verb in such a long sentence agrees with the subject.

Examples:

The complex *interaction* among humans, their by-products, and sensitive ecosystems *needs* to be examined.

Wrap-up

- **Some nouns look plural and aren't** — *physics, mathematics, economics, news*, for example. Each of them is singular.

- **Some nouns look plural and are** — These have no singular form. Some well-known ones are *proceeds, goods, scissors*.

- **Some nouns don't look plural, but are** — *media* (the singular form is *medium*), *criteria* (the singular form is *criterion*), *data*. (The singular form is *datum*. But so many people have used a singular verb with "data" that it is now permissible to treat the word as either singular or plural. Check the custom in the company you work for.)

- **Some nouns look plural, but can be either singular or plural** — *series*. Whether it is plural or singular depends upon whether you are talking about one series or two or more series. (There's only one World *Series*, isn't there? Unless, of course, you've watched all the World *Series* [PLURAL] since Hack Wilson played for the Cubs.)

- **Phrases or clauses, instead of nouns, can be subjects of sentences** — When they are subjects they are almost always singular. Some examples:

    Cleaning the house is not my favorite hobby.
    Whether he is right or wrong is beside the point.
    What this country needs is a 50–cent cup of coffee.

- **"The number" vs. "a number"** — When *"the* number" is the subject of a sentence, use a singular verb. But when "a number" is the subject of a sentence, use a plural verb. For example:

    The number of people who have trouble with subjects and verbs *is* large. BUT A number of the problems with subjects and verbs *are* easy to solve.

- **Subjects that are periods of time, amounts of money, and quantities** — These may be either singular or plural, depending upon whether the subject refers to a total amount or to a number of individual units. This one example will give you the idea:

    Six months *is* a long time to wait for a new car.
    ("Six months" is here one chunk of time, so it's singular.)

    Six months *have* gone by since I ordered my car.
    ("Six months" here refers to the number of months, so the subject is plural.)

LET'S TRY! 2-2

Correct the following sentences so that subjects and verbs are in agreement.

0. Nothing any of us has suggested seem[s] to make any difference to her.

1. Every one of the plates ~~are~~ [is] chipped or cracked.

2. Two dollars ~~are~~ [is] a lot to pay for an ice cream bar, but Dream bars are worth it.

3. The fine for overdue books ~~are~~ [is] five cents a day.

4. A few miles beyond the intersection of Bridge and Thompson ~~are~~ [is] a bunch of fast-food restaurants.

5. Neither Dad nor his brothers ~~was~~ [were] able to go to college.

6. The results of a questionnaire circulated throughout the department indicate[s] that some of the staff wishe[s] they could skip the company picnic and just have the day off instead.

7. She said most of the sentences in my report to the Grievance Committee need[s] to be shortened.

8. Anybody with that many charge cards ~~are~~ [is] just asking for trouble.

9. Bill or Jake ~~have~~ [has] offered to drive us home after the meeting.

10. The memo said the canned goods ~~is~~ [are] to be taken to the loading dock before the end of the workday on Friday.

11. I heard that Jean and maybe Paula, too, ~~has~~ [have] signed up for the course.

(12.) Before all the publicity about the dangers of salt and cholesterol, ham and eggs ~~were~~ [was] famous as an all-American dish.

13. The media ~~is~~ [are] having a field day with the rumors all his former colleagues at the agency ~~is~~ [are] spreading about him.

14. The number of responses we received to the special mailing ~~were~~ [was] disappointing, to say the least.

15. Whether to take more courses in English or in economics ~~are~~ [is] something I have to decide.

(Check your work in the Correct Markings *section at the back of this book.)*

(TEMPLATE USERS: Complete this exercise using your template disk.)

Class Exercise 2-1

Directions: Proofread the following sentences for errors in subject-verb agreement, and make the changes necessary to correct the sentences.

Almost everybody associate~~s~~ the invention of printing with a fifteenth-century German named Johannes Gutenberg, but the details of his life ~~is~~ *are* by no means certain. Some historians who ~~has~~ *have* studied the matter say~~s~~ he may or may not have been the first person in Europe to print with movable type; but none of them question the importance of the invention, which quickly replaced the arduous, time-consuming methods of reproducing text that ~~was~~ *were* used up to that time. The days of pages carved by hand on wooden blocks and manuscripts beautifully illuminated by monks and other copyists working with a brush or a quill ~~was~~ *were* soon over.

With the new technology, all the letters and other characters that ~~was~~ *were* needed to copy a manuscript ~~was~~ *were* individually cast in molds, arranged in text lines by hand, and locked into forms representing the pages of the finished book. After the number of copies needed ~~were~~ *was* printed, every letter and punctuation mark ~~were~~ *was* separated, sorted, and stored in two cases awaiting the next job. The upper of the two cases ~~were~~ *was* for capital letters, the lower for small letters. (Sound familiar? Even though no one except hobbyists set~~s~~ type by hand any more, we still call capitals uppercase and small letters lowercase.)

(TEMPLATE USERS: Complete this exercise using your template disk.)

JOB READY? You should be ready to do Job Sheets 8* and 9 now!

Subjects vs. Objects

Not every sentence contains objects.
Remember that definition of a sentence: "A sentence is a group of words with at least a subject and a verb ... that expresses a complete thought."

But when the verb tells of some action that affects someone or something, that person or thing is the object of the action, and a sentence with such a verb contains an object.

Nouns as Objects

Here's a sentence that has a noun as an object:

DOG BITES MAN

A famous newspaper editor once said that this sentence would not make a good headline because it wasn't really news. Dogs bite mail carriers and joggers frequently. But the following headline would be news:

MAN BITES DOG

In the first sentence, "dog" is the subject, "bites" is the verb, and "man" is the object. The dog (the subject) *performs* the action of the verb ("bites"). The man (the object) *receives* the action of the verb ("bites"). (Poor man.)

But in the second sentence, the man *performs* the biting and the dog *receives* the bite. "Man" becomes the subject, and "dog" becomes the object.

You can usually tell very easily when nouns are subjects or objects. They don't change form ("man" is still "man," and "dog" is still "dog"). But they do change positions relative to the verb. The subject comes before the verb and the object comes after the verb in most English sentences.

Pronouns as Objects

Personal pronouns are not so easy. Personal pronouns (see Table 2-2) change form depending upon many things, including changing form as objects.

TABLE 2-2   Forms of Personal Pronouns

Subjects	Objects
I	Me
You (singular)	You
He	Him
She	Her
It	It
We	Us
You (plural)	You
They	Them
Who	Whom
Whoever	Whomever
Whosoever	Whomsoever

If "he" is the subject, and "hit" is the verb, then the object cannot be *I, he, she, it, we, they, who, whoever,* or *whosoever*; those are all subjects. If "he" is hitting another person, and you are using a personal pronoun for that person, "he" can "hit" only *me, you, him, her, it, us, you, them, whom, whomever, or whomsoever*. Those are the **objects** and are the only forms that can **receive** the action of the verb—namely, the "hit." If you don't know the subjective forms and the objective forms of the personal pronouns, learn them. Knowledge of them, and knowledge that objects are the words in a sentence that receive the action of the verb, will help you catch many errors as you proofread.

JOB READY? You should be ready to do Job Sheet 10* now!

Three Kinds of Objects

Three kinds of objects can be found in sentences—DIRECT OBJECTS, OBJECTS OF PREPOSITIONS, and INDIRECT OBJECTS.

Direct Objects

In the sentence, *The rain flooded the house*, "rain" is the subject; "flooded" is the verb; and "house" is the object. It's very straightforward—RAIN FLOODED HOUSE. The object "house" is a DIRECT object.

Objects of Prepositions

In the sentence, *The book was written by him*, "book" is the subject, "was written" is the verb, and "him" is an object — but not a direct object. It relates to the preposition "by." It's an object of a preposition. It's still an object, but what's a preposition?

A **preposition** is a word that shows the relationship of some noun or pronoun to a verb — usually a verb that precedes it. For instance, in that good patriotic phrase *Made in America*, "in" is a preposition. It shows where (that's the relationship) something was "Made" (the verb).

Many words are used as prepositions. They are usually short ("between" is about the longest of them). You know them well, because they occur frequently when we write or talk. Keep in mind that these words are not always used as prepositions; sometimes one of them may function as a verb, an adjective, or an adverb. But here are many of the words that are usually prepositions: *of, by, for, from, to, with, over, under, about, after, at, between, among, as, in, within, without*. The important thing for a proofreader to know is that they are always followed by objects.

If you see a word that can be used as a preposition, you know that the noun or pronoun following it is an object. When that following word is a personal pronoun, you know it must have a certain form — namely, the objective form.

If you see *"between you and I,"* you know that is wrong. "Between" is a preposition and "I" is a subject form. It has to be the object form, "me." The correct phrase is *"between you and me."*

Indirect Objects

Look at this sentence: *Robert gave his dog a bath.*

"Robert" is the subject; "gave" is the verb. What about "dog" and "bath"? Which is the object? The answer is: both are objects. The direct object is "bath"; that's what "Robert gave." "Dog" is an indirect object; a preposition is understood, even though it is not expressed before "dog," and the sentence really means *Robert gave [to] his dog a bath,* or *Robert gave a bath [to] his dog.*

Indirect objects are really the same as objects of prepositions, except that the preposition may not be expressed. In proofreading, if you see a sentence of this form, figure out what the direct object is by identifying the result of the verb's action. Then see if you can mentally insert a "to" or "for" in front of the other word that seems to be an object; if you can and it makes sense, you know you have an indirect object.

As a proofreader, you need to know whether personal pronouns in a sentence are objects or subjects. It doesn't matter whether they are direct or indirect objects, or objects of prepositions; they change form, and must be in the correct objective form. Watch for personal pronouns.

He is a man (who)(whom) I never met. Which personal pronoun should it be? *[whom]*

He hired (she)(her). Which personal pronoun should it be? *[her]*

The argument was between (he)(him) and (she)(her). Which should it be? *[him] [her]* or *[them]*

33

> **LET'S TRY!** 2-3

Mark personal pronouns to put them in the correct subject or object form.

0. Of who[m] do you speak? H[im] or her?

1. Between you and I [me], the manager is proud of she [her] and I [me].

2. I don't know whom [who] is going to the convention.

3. The doctor gave he [him] a clean bill of health.

4. To Who[m] It May Concern:

5. The argument was between him and she [her].

(Check your work in the Correct Markings section at the back of this book.)

(TEMPLATE USERS: Complete this exercise using your template disk.)

▼ Class Exercise 2-2

Directions: Proofread and correct the following text, which contains errors in the use of forms of pronouns and in subject-verb agreement.

This will be a quick fax to tell you I finally got an answer from he [him] and Dexter about next month's meeting. They want you and I [me] to work up a tentative schedule. Half of the information them [those] two guys sent us earlier have [has] been changed, so you and me [I have] has to start pretty much from scratch. Just between you and I [me], nobody in my department except Nikki and I have [has] given this much thought—and her and her family is [are] leaving on vacation Friday. I don't know anybody here whom [who] is able to help, so I guess it's up to we [us] two to run with it. All I know that I didn't tell you earlier are [is] that the videos Jackie Dombek took at the regional meetings is [are] available if anybody want[s] to use them. You and me [I] have lots to talk about. I'll call you tomorrow.

(TEMPLATE USERS: Complete this exercise using your template disk.)

JOB READY? You should be ready to do Job Sheet 11 now!

The Final Silent E Spelling Rule

1. **The first half of the rule:** If you have a word that ends with a silent *e* (such as *love*), and you want to add a suffix that begins with a vowel, DROP the final *e* of the word before adding the suffix.

    Examples: *love + ing* becomes *loving*; *move + able* becomes *movable*; *sterile + ize* becomes *sterilize*; *rare + ity* becomes *rarity*.

   Now for the exceptions to the first part of the rule:

   a. Sometimes you must KEEP an *e* that would normally be dropped, simply so that readers don't get the word confused with another word.

      Examples: *Dye + ing = dyeing* (not to be confused with dying); *singe + ing = singeing* (not to be confused with singing).

   b. Sometimes you must KEEP an *e* that would normally be dropped, simply to make sure that words with a *c* or *g* before the *e* are pronounced with a SOFT sound. (NOTE: "Soft sound" means the *c* is pronounced as *s*, and the *g* is pronounced as *j*. See also "The Final CE or GE Spelling Rule," Lesson 5.)

      Examples: *notice + able = noticeable* but *notice + ing = noticing*; *manage + able = manageable* but *manage + ing = managing*

   c. Sometimes you may take your choice. Apparently, nobody ever fitted these words to a rule. You may use *likeable* or *likable*, *saleable* or *salable*, *useable* or *usable*, *sizeable* or *sizable*.

2. **The second half of the rule:** Keep the final *e* if the suffix begins with a consonant.

    Examples: *sure + ly* becomes *surely*; *case + ment* becomes *casement*; *polite + ness* becomes *politeness*, *spite + ful* becomes *spiteful*; *awe + some* becomes *awesome*.

   Now for exceptions to the second part of the rule:

   a. In American English, you drop the *e* after a *dg* when the suffix begins with a consonant.

      Examples: *judge + ment = judgment*; *abridge + ment = abridgment*; *acknowledge + ment = acknowledgment*.

   b. The words *argument*, *truly*, and *awful* follow no rule. You just have to learn them!

LET'S TRY! 2-4

Find and correct with proper proofreader's marks the words that disobey the Final Silent E Spelling Rule.

0. The spit**e**ful man had to steril**i**ze all his dishes.

1. He was absolut**e**ly aws**e**ome when he played his guitar.

2. "I was only jok~~e~~ing," said Julio, typ**e**ing his memoirs.

3. The chef was bak~~e~~ing in the bak**e**ry, wiggl~~e~~ing his fingers.

4. He let out a pierc~~e~~ing scream. It was very notic**e**able.

5. Chen Li's greatest achiev**e**ment was mak~~e~~ing money.

(Check your work in the Correct Markings *section at the back of this book.)*

(TEMPLATE USERS: Complete this exercise using your template disk.)

JOB READY? You should be able to do Job Sheet 12 now!

Lesson 3

Proofreading for Commas, Semicolons, Spelling

When you complete this Lesson, you will be able to achieve the following objectives:

▶ ***Objective Number 13:*** Proofread, using correct proofreader's marks, text containing errors in the four uses of commas, the two uses of semicolons, a misspelling, and a misuse of a pronoun form. Performance standard: 90 percent

▶ ***Objective Number 14*:*** Match with 100 percent accuracy six comma and semicolon rules to ten properly punctuated sentences by placing the number of the appropriate rule in the blank preceding each sentence.

▶ ***Objective Number 15:*** Spell correctly 80 percent of an orally given list of words that follow the Final Y Spelling Rule and are exceptions to the Final Y Spelling Rule.

▶ ***Objective Number 16:*** Spell correctly 80 percent of an orally given list of words that follow the Change for Plural Spelling Rules and are exceptions to the Change for Plural Rules.

Punctuation I

Why does English have to have all those dots, squiggles, and curlicues we call "punctuation"? Read the example, and you may see why.

Example:

Short words are words of might this observation wise but not truer than most generalizations does not imply that long words should never be used it does suggest that long words are more likely than short ones to be artificial affected and pretentious the user of jargon will write the answer is in the negative rather than no

Now read the same passage with the proper punctuation:

Example:

"Short words are words of might." This observation — wise but no truer than most generalizations — does not imply that long words should never be used; it does suggest that long words are more likely than short ones to be artificial, affected, and pretentious. The user of jargon will write "The answer is in the negative" rather than "No."[1]

Punctuation both joins and separates sentences and parts of sentences. It is necessary because it helps us understand what our language means.

The most frequently used punctuation mark is the comma. Look at the difference commas can make in the meaning of this sentence. Here it is without commas:

Example:

The Democrats say the Republicans are sure to win the election.

That ought to make the Republicans happy, but now look at the same sentence with commas added (probably added by a Democrat):

Example:

The Democrats, say the Republicans, are sure to win the election.

Two little commas have reversed the meaning simply by SEPARATING three words from the rest of the sentence.

Commas — What Do They Do?

Commas SEPARATE certain parts of sentences from one another *within the sentence*. The separating they do is not strong, but it helps a reader figure out the meaning of a sentence. A comma separation is not nearly so strong as that of a semicolon, a colon, a question mark, an

---

[1] Shaw, Harry, *Errors in English and Ways To Correct Them* (Third Edition), New York, Perennial Library, Harper & Row, 1986, p. 47.

exclamation point, or a period, but it is strong enough to affect meaning. Before learning the right places for commas to do their job of separating, try putting commas in the right places in the paragraph below. Put commas in it now; they're the only punctuation marks that are missing.

Example:

```
The old boat which was painted red sails every
Sunday from the crowded marina where when not
sailing it docks next to numerous newer boats
painted mostly blue or green not red.
```

The answer: The old boat, which was painted red, sails every Sunday from the crowded marina where, when not sailing, it docks next to numerous newer boats, painted mostly blue or green, not red.

The Four Uses of Commas

So that you can have a good understanding of different situations covered by four basic uses of the comma, here are examples of ways each may appear when you proofread.

COMMA USE N0. 1: Commas separate "not-*absolutely*-necessary" elements from the rest of the sentence.

A. The "not-*absolutely*-necessary" introductory word or phrase

Example:

Yes, we have no bananas.

Analysis: The part of the sentence that is really necessary is *we have no bananas*. The word "Yes" is just an emphasis or attention-getter, and if it were left out, the sentence would still have its essential original meaning. So, although the word "Yes" does add emphasis and gain attention, IT IS NOT ABSOLUTELY NECESSARY. Therefore, it should be separated from the sentence by the use of a comma.

B. The "not-*absolutely*-necessary" definition of a subject or object (called an appositive)

Example:

Joan Fortesque, the lawyer, won all her cases.

Analysis: The essential meaning of the sentence is that Joan Fortesque won all her cases. The words "the lawyer" do not change the essential meaning of the sentence. THEY ARE NOT ABSOLUTELY NECESSARY, even though they do define what Joan Fortesque does for a living. Therefore, "the lawyer" should be separated from the rest of the sentence by commas.

C. The "not-*absolutely*-necessary" word or phrase that interrupts the flow of the sentence

Example:

He told me, however, that he had no money.

Analysis: The essential meaning of this sentence is that he told me he had no money. The word "however" does indicate that something else had been said earlier that did not lead me to suspect that he was out of money, but "however" interrupts the flow, and doesn't change the essential meaning of the sentence. IT IS NOT ABSOLUTELY NECESSARY. Therefore, it should be separated from the rest of the sentence by commas.

D. The "not-*absolutely*-necessary" clause (called a non-restrictive clause)

Example:

The boat, which was painted red, sailed well.

Analysis: All the sentence really says is that the boat sailed well. The fact that it was painted red is just additional, nice-to-know information about the boat. IT IS NOT ABSOLUTELY NECESSARY to the essential meaning of the sentence. Therefore, "which was painted red" should be separated from the rest of the sentence by commas.

▶ **A PROOFREADING TIP** ◀

Most clauses that begin with WHICH are nonrestrictive, or not-absolutely-necessary, and should be separated by commas. Clauses that begin with THAT, however, are usually restrictive, or essential to the meaning of the basic sentence, and should not be separated by commas.

E. The "not-*absolutely*-necessary" use of a name at the beginning, in the midst, or at the end of a sentence to indicate to whom the writer or speaker is communicating directly (called "direct address")

Example:

Please go to the store, Lisa, and get me an apple. or
Lisa, please go to the store and get me an apple. or
Please go to the store and get me an apple, Lisa.

Analysis: The main idea is that "I" want somebody to get me an apple. "I" addressed my request to Lisa, but "I" could have just looked at her, or assumed that she would be the one to do it. The name, "Lisa," is not absolutely necessary here. Therefore, it should be separated by commas.

COMMA USE NO. 2: Commas separate elements of a series, including the last element of the series preceded by "and."

A. Subjects in a series

Example:

The father, his wife, his son, and his two daughters boarded the plane.

Analysis: "Father," "wife," "son," and "daughters" in series are the compound subject of the sentence and should be separated by commas.

B. Verbs in a series
Example:

Sandra washed, dressed, ate breakfast, and put papers into her briefcase.

Analysis: This is a series of actions taken by Sandra. The commas help understanding.

C. Objects in a series
Example:

The muggers bruised his arms, legs, head, neck, stomach, and back.

Analysis: Every word in the series is in answer to "What did they bruise?" Therefore, this is a series of direct objects.

D. Phrases in a series
Example:

this government of the people, by the people, and for the people

Analysis: Here are Lincoln's three famous prepositional phrases. A series of prepositional phrases is separated by commas.

E. Clauses in a series
Example:

The house that Jack built, that Jill bought, that Jill's husband sold, and that Jack finally inherited was palatial.

Analysis: These are all restrictive clauses—absolutely necessary and beginning with "that"—but they are in a series, so they must be separated from one another with commas.

F. Adjectives in a series
Example:

The tall, dark, muscular, and handsome man won the race.

Analysis: When commas separate all the characteristics of this man, they make each characteristic stand out all the more.

G. Adverbs in a series
Example:

The cellist played expertly, rapidly, feelingly, and beautifully.

Analysis: The cellist's many abilities show up much more prominently when the serial commas are inserted.

You have seen several examples of the use of commas in a series of subjects, verbs, objects, phrases, clauses, adjectives, and adverbs. Now you're ready to learn how commas are used when you have two sentences within a sentence (clauses) connected with conjunctions such as *and, or, nor, for,* and *but,* or when one clause is dependent upon the other.

COMMA USE NO. 3: Commas separate two independent clauses joined by a conjunction (and, for, or, nor, but) when the subject is stated in both clauses, and commas separate a dependent clause from a main clause.

Remember that clauses are really like sentences within sentences. A clause contains a noun or a pronoun as a subject, it contains a verb, and it may contain a direct object.

A. Independent clauses
Example:

He took a bite of the cake, and he decided he liked it.

Analysis: Notice that there's an "and" in the middle of the sentence. That separates the two independent clauses somewhat, but, since the subject "he" is repeated after the "and," a comma should be inserted before the "and" to separate the clauses.

But what if the sentence read like this?

Example:

He took a bite of the cake and decided he liked it.

Analysis: Now a comma isn't necessary. There is no stated subject after the "and," so there is no second independent clause. Instead, now you have a sentence with one clause and two verbs. There's nothing to separate.

B. Dependent and main clauses

When the first of two clauses begins with *if, when, although, after, since, until,* or any other word that limits the meaning of the verb in that clause, such a clause is DEPENDENT. The dependent clause must be separated from the other clause (the main or independent clause) by inserting a comma.

Example:

If the limousine doesn't arrive in time, I'll miss my plane.

Analysis: The clause beginning with "if" begins the sentence and would not stand alone as a sentence even though it has a subject *(limousine)* and a verb *(doesn't arrive)*. Its status as a clause depends on the main clause *(I'll miss my plane)* which can stand alone as a sentence. The "if" clause is dependent on the main clause, and the comma must separate the two clauses. If the clauses were reversed in order—*I'll miss my plane if the limousine doesn't arrive in time*—and if you can easily understand the whole sentence without the comma, modern usage allows you to omit the comma that separates dependent clauses from main clauses. Then the comma is optional.

COMMA USE NO. 4: Commas separate direct quotations from the rest of the sentence.

You find this comma used in fiction mostly, but once in a while businesses and institutions must quote directly what somebody said. Here are two examples that could appear in a business document:

Examples:

As our CEO so wisely said, "Our customers come first." OR "Our customers come first," said our CEO.

Analysis: Notice that when the unquoted material comes before the quotation, the comma precedes the quotation mark. When the quotation comes first, the comma is inside the ending quotation mark.

And remember that a quotation that is not a direct quote doesn't need a comma before it to separate it.

Examples:

NOT A DIRECT QUOTE: Tom said he enjoyed reading *Investment Strategy*.

A DIRECT QUOTE: Tom said, "I enjoy reading *Investment Strategy*."

LET'S TRY!

3-1

Insert or delete missing or misplaced commas.

0. Patricia was remarkable: She was beautiful, intelligent, hard-working, honest, and rich.

1. Yes, I think we should go to the concert.

2. Curly, the clown, is the funniest person I ever saw.

3. The boss' secretary, however, wouldn't let the applicant enter the door.

4. The automobile, which had just had a brake job, could stop on a dime.

5. Would you please make 25 copies of this, Melissa?

6. Yes, the colorful float, which took a year to decorate, won the prize.

7. Tom, Dick, and Harry all like to ride, hunt, and fish.

8. The automobile that is quiet, that gives good gasoline mileage, that has enough power to climb hills, that has a good warranty, and that has dual airbags is the one to buy.

9. She also plays the drums rhythmically, expertly, and loudly.

10. I went to the mall, and I bought a shirt.

11. I went to the mall and bought a shirt.

12. Successful retail stores say their attitude is that their customers come first.

13. "I'm ready to go," said Ashley.

14. The article in *Golf Tips*, the magazine, was entitled, "How To Swing."

(Check your work in the Correct Markings *section at the back of this book.)*

(TEMPLATE USERS: Complete this exercise using your template disk.)

Class Exercise 3-1

Directions: Insert missing commas or delete wrongly placed commas in the following text. All the errors in this text are errors in the four comma uses you have learned from the preceding pages. Proofread this on your own.

As everybody in today's business world or almost everybody, probably knows by now, "fax," short for "facsimile," is a system for transmitting photographs and documents by electronic means. Though it's just in the last decade that fax machines have been sprouting like dandelions on office desks, in shopping malls, and even at the tops of ski hills, faxing is not a new technology. For five decades, give or take a decade or two, news wire services, law enforcement agencies, and weather bureaus have been using fax to transmit images all over the United States.

The great advantage of fax transmission, in addition to its speed, is that it can send typed documents as well as handwritten text, graphs, photographs, drawings, and other types of hard copy. Let's suppose, for example, that you're on the phone with a vendor who tells you the office furniture you ordered is going to be delivered that afternoon. You're going to have to be out of the office, unfortunately, on a sales call, but you don't want to delay the delivery, so you say, "The new desk goes under the far window, the bookcase fits beside the tan chair, the work table sits at right angles to the desk, and..."

"Hey, wait a minute," he interrupts. "Why don't you just fax me a floor plan?"

Now, about that word "facsimile." Well, it entered the language when Thomas Fuller, a seventeenth-century clergyman and author, spliced two Latin words together—"fac," which means "make," and "simile," which means "like." The ability of fax transmission to "make like" or, in other words, to send copies that are true to the original accounts for its popularity as a tool of communication. When Fuller used the word, however, it wasn't a compliment; he used it to describe the prose of some of his fellow writers, those who don't have any original ideas of their own and copy from other people.

(TEMPLATE USERS: Complete this exercise using your template disk.)

Semicolons — What Do They Do?

Semicolons do two things:

1. They mark the point of balance between two contrasting or parallel independent clauses that are not connected by a conjunction *(and, or, nor, for, but)*. Remember, an independent clause is really a sentence within a sentence.
2. They act as "super-commas" in series in which the elements of the series already contain commas.

The Semicolon as a Balancer

Let's put a famous statement on a teeter-totter.

To err is human to forgive is divine.

Notice that this is really two sentences. The meaning of the first part is: *It is human to make errors*. The meaning of the second part is: *It is divine (God-like) to forgive errors*.

The two parts of the sentence are balanced. There is no *and, or, nor, for,* or *but* between the two parts. A semicolon should be placed between them. It acts as a fulcrum on a teeter-totter – the point where the weight on each side is the same, the place that will make the two parts balance.

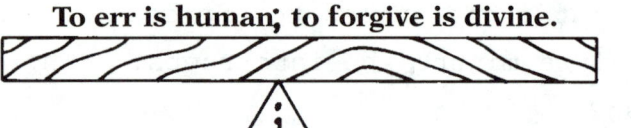

To err is human; to forgive is divine.

Now the scale is in balance. Here are some other sentences that are perfect for semicolons:

Examples:

Art is long; life is brief.—*Virgil*

Error is the force that welds men together; truth is communicated to men only by deeds of truth.—*Leo Tolstoy*

Jeanette studied hard; she made the Honor Roll.

Learn a lot; earn a lot.

Words That Signal "Semicolon"

When you, as a proofreader, see the following words, you can be almost certain that you have a sentence with two independent clauses that are balanced. These words usually begin the second clause. If you see one of them, make certain that a semicolon is in front of it (and usually that there is a comma after it):

accordingly	consequently	in addition	nevertheless
also	furthermore	indeed	still
anyhow	hence	likewise	then
besides	however	moreover	therefore

though

Examples:

Joe was tired; <u>nevertheless</u>, he passed for a touchdown.
Last year was profitable; <u>consequently</u>, we'll issue bonuses.
We'll pay bonuses; <u>moreover</u>, we'll raise salaries.
He made his boss angry; <u>still</u>, he got a raise.
I did all my assignments; <u>besides</u>, I did some extra projects.

You get the idea. Those words will signal to you: "Aha! We need a semicolon here!"

The Semicolon as Super-Comma

The other use of the semicolon is to act as a *super-comma* in a series in which at least one of the elements of the series contains commas.

Example:

IN A SERIES OF DATES:

The four meetings he attended were on November 12, 1990; February 10, 1991; September 14, 1992; and January 6, 1993.

Example:

IN A SERIES OF CITY AND STATE NAMES:

Anke's long trip took her to New York, New York; London, England; Geneva, Switzerland; Riyadh, Saudi Arabia; and, finally, back to New York City.

Example:

IN A SERIES OF COMPOUND SUBJECTS
THAT CONTAIN COMMAS:

The quick, brown fox; the slow, green turtle; and the fuzzy, white rabbit had an exciting race.

Let's Try! 3-2

Insert, delete, or substitute missing or misplaced semicolons or commas.

0. The only times the concert artist could appear were on January 6, 1990; February 12, 1991; March 3, 1992; April 12, 1993; May 23, 1994; and June 10, 1995.

1. Buy the workbook; borrow the textbook.

2. Kieran was a very serious person; accordingly, he never laughed at jokes.

3. Maria inadvertently missed the bus, but she got a ride with Jeanne.

4. Maria inadvertently missed the bus; still, she got a ride.

5. The party lost faith in their candidate; they decided to vote for someone else.

6. Pete, the plumber; Elena, the electrician; Carlos, the carpenter; and Paola, the plasterer, formed a company to build inexpensive houses.

7. Let's see America! First, Boston, Massachusetts; then New York City; then Washington, DC; then Detroit, Michigan; then Chicago, Illinois; then Santa Fe, New Mexico; then San Francisco, California; then Tucson, Arizona; then New Orleans, Louisiana; and end up in Miami, Florida.

(Check your work in the Correct Markings *section at the back of this book.)*

(TEMPLATE USERS: Complete this exercise using your template disk.)

Class Exercise 3-2

Directions: Insert missing semicolons and commas or delete wrongly placed semicolons and commas in the following text, using rules presented in Lesson 3.

Alistair Booker, our representative, attended only four meetings of the assembly: November 12, 1988; February 10, 1989; September 14, 1989; and January 6, 1990.

As a result, his constituents lost faith in him; they decided to vote for someone else. The problem, however, was that nobody else was as qualified as Alistair; they didn't know whom else to vote for. His constituents were in a quandary; they didn't know what to do.

Just when they had come to the conclusion that they would have to vote for him anyway, though, Alistair himself came to their rescue. He told them he could not run for election again; they would have to get someone else.

Now his constituents had to find someone to replace him; moreover, they had to find someone who would attend more meetings. Consequently, they chose a relatively unknown member, Jane Salazar, to replace Alistair as representative.

As it turned out, Jane, unbeknown to the constituents, was more qualified than Alistair and attended all the meetings; the constituents were pleased with the wisdom of their choice.

(TEMPLATE USERS: Complete this exercise using your template disk.)

JOB READY? You should be ready to do Job Sheets 13 and 14* now!

The Final Y Spelling Rule

1. If you have a word that ends in *y*, and if the *y* is preceded by a *consonant*, change the *y* to *i* before adding a suffix, unless the suffix begins with an *i*.

Examples:

plenty + *ful* becomes *plentiful*   *heavy* + *ness* becomes *heaviness*
hierarchy + *cal* becomes *hierarchical*   *baby* + *es* becomes *babies*

BUT NOTICE WHAT HAPPENS WHEN THE SUFFIX BEGINS WITH *I*

baby + *ing* becomes *babying*   *lobby* + *ist* becomes *lobbyist*

2. What if there's a *vowel* in front of the final *y*? For most words with a vowel before the *y*, you do not change the *y* to *i*. You simply add the suffix.

Examples:

obey + *ed* becomes *obeyed*   *chimney* + *s* becomes *chimneys*

Now, for the exceptions:

lay-laid   say-said   gay-gaily   day-daily   slay-slain   pay-paid

(Some of these are irregular verb forms, but verb endings can be considered as suffixes. They all have an "ay" sound. It may help you remember.)

Some Final Y Words with which you can break the rule or not as you wish:

Examples:

shy   can be *shier* or *shyer*; *shiest* or *shyest*.
dry   can be *drily* or *dryly*; *drier* or *dryer*.
fly   can be *flier* or *flyer*.

> **LET'S TRY!** 3-3
>
> Find and correct the words in the following paragraph that disobey the Final Y Spelling Rule.
>
> ```
> It's high time I conveyd my thanks to you for the beautyful
> party. I had to leave earlyer than I wanted to because of pressing
> busyness dutys (a meeting with some lobbyists and their
> attornies), but not before I'd payed a visit to the bountyful
> buffet table; admired the artistic bouquets of daisys, baby's
> breath, peonys, and lilys of the valley; and happyly sampled the
> elegant grocerys layed out there. When I described the spread to
> Margaret—roast beef, lobster rolls, candyed apples, and not just
> one but two smoked turkies—she sayed, "Everybody knows that your
> abilitys at giving partys are unmatched."
> ```
>
> *(Check your work in the Correct Markings section at the back of this book.)*
>
> (TEMPLATE USERS: Complete this exercise using your template disk.)

▼ The Change for Plural Spelling Rules

First, know that the plurals of most nouns in English are formed simply by adding an *s* at the end. But here are some exceptions and variations you should know:

1. See the Final Y Spelling Rule on the previous page. To make a plural of a word that ends in *y* when the *y* is preceded by a consonant, you must change the *y* to *i* and add *es* as the suffix. Notice the examples: *battery* becomes *batteries*, *rivalry* becomes *rivalries*, *fury* becomes *furies*, *daisy* becomes *daisies*, *ruby* becomes *rubies*, etc. And, as in the Final Y Rule, if the noun ending in *y* has a vowel preceding the *y*, simply add an *s* at its end: *turkeys, attorneys, jetways, soliloquys, alloys*.
2. Nouns that end in *sis* in the singular become plural if you change the *sis* to *ses*. *Analysis* becomes *analyses*; *crisis* becomes *crises*; *basis* becomes *bases*.
3. Singular nouns that end in soft sounds such as *s, sh, ch, x*, or *z* must have *es* added to form their plurals: *miss* becomes *misses*; *wish* becomes *wishes*; *church* becomes *churches*; *tax* becomes *taxes*; *buzz* becomes *buzzes*.

4. Singular nouns that end in *o* with a consonant before the *o* must usually add an *es* to form the plural: *tomato* becomes *tomatoes*; *potato* becomes *potatoes*; *halo* becomes *haloes*. BUT if a vowel precedes the *o*, just an *s* makes it plural: *video* becomes *videos*; *radio* becomes *radios*; *rodeo* becomes *rodeos*; *tattoo* becomes *tattoos*.
(The plurals of musical terms ending in *o*, such as *solo, alto, soprano,* are exceptions. So is *taco*. To these exceptions, you add just the *s* to form the plural.)
5. Some nouns don't change from the singular to the plural. Look at *deer, sheep, moose, scissors*, for example; you never saw a "scissor," did you? These you just have to learn. They are exceptions.
6. And, finally, there are some words that have strange forms for the plural. *Ox* becomes *oxen*; *goose* becomes *geese*; *mouse* becomes *mice*. (That does not mean that the plural for *spouse* is *spice*!)

Let's Try!   3-4

Find and correct with proper proofreader's marks the unusual plural forms of certain words using the Change for Plural Spelling Rules.
(NOTE: The first line has been correctly marked as an example.)

The rivalr*ies* that crop up among chemists who do chemical analyses really have no solid bases. And they aren't really battles between the sexes, even though the numbers of men and women among such chemists are about equal. Instead, the frequent crises occur simply because the criteria for analysis differ so much among them. And each chemist, of course, thinks he or she is correct; so correct, in fact, that you would think they all had haloes around their heads. Still, their data are different, and their mediums of communication are mixed. To evaluate them truly, one must study carefully the appendices of their many books.

(Check your work in the Correct Markings *section at the back of this book.*)

 (TEMPLATE USERS: Complete this exercise using your template disk.)

JOB READY? You should be ready to do Job Sheets 15 and 16 now.

Lesson 4

Proofreading for Periods, Questions, Exclamations, Parentheses, Dashes, Brackets, Colons, Spelling

When you complete this Lesson, you will be able to achieve the following objectives:

▶ ***Objective Number 17:*** Proofread, using correct proofreader's marks, given text containing errors in the use or non-use of commas, semicolons, and periods as enders, abbreviators, and decimals. Performance standard: 95 percent.

▶ ***Objective Number 18*:*** Insert or delete, using correct proofreader's marks, missing or wrongly placed commas, semicolons, periods, question marks, exclamation points, colons, and dashes, and correct spelling errors in given text. Performance standard: 95 percent.

▶ ***Objective Number 19:*** Proofread, using correct proofreader's marks, given text containing errors in the use of parentheses and dashes, as well as question marks, exclamation points, and colons. Performance standard: 100 percent.

▶ ***Objective Number 20*:*** Proofread, using correct proofreader's marks, given text containing errors in subject-verb agreement, the use of plural forms, spelling, and punctuation involving commas, semicolons, periods, parentheses, question marks, exclamation points, colons, and dashes. Performance standard: 100 percent.

▶ ***Objective Number 21:*** Spell correctly 80 percent of an orally given list of words that follow the Double Consonant Spelling Rule and exceptions to the Double Consonant Spelling Rule.

Punctuation II

The first part of this Lesson is about punctuation that tells you when you've reached the end of a sentence—periods, question marks, and exclamation points. These marks have other uses, too, but ending sentences is their most frequent function.

The next part of the Lesson is about punctuation that fences off parts of a sentence from the rest of that sentence for various reasons.

The last part of the Lesson is about colons, which act as announcers of something coming up.

And, as usual, there's a new spelling rule.

It's interesting to realize that the little squiggles that make punctuation marks can act as stoppers, as fences, and as announcers. Punctuation marks are almost a language in themselves.

Periods – What Do They Do?

The British call the *period* a "full stop." That's a good name for it, because the most important and frequent use of the period is to bring a sentence to a full stop.

But that's not the only thing a period can do. The period has three uses:

1. A period marks the end of a sentence.

Example:

My new computer should be installed tomorrow.

2. A period is used as a decimal point.

Examples:

The average family consists of 2.3 people and 3.6 pets.
I paid $14.98 for that tie; it's probably worth only $2.00.

The main thing to remember is that there should not be a space either before or after the decimal point (period).

3. A period is used after most abbreviations.

As a reminder, here are some common abbreviations with their periods:

ft.	etc.	Mr.	Mrs.	Ms.	Dr.	Jan.	Feb.	D.C.	f.o.b.
a.m.	p.m.	M.A.	B.C.	Sr.	Jr.	Mon.	Wed.	Bldg.	Illus.

But some abbreviations are so familiar that we no longer use periods with them:

| CBS | NBC | ABC | CIA | GNP | IOU | FBI | PR |
| SOS | UN | IQ | NYSE | MIT | LSU | R&D | UCLA |

Of course, there are the official two-letter abbreviations for state names that the post office wants us to use which don't use periods. The list of state abreviations can be found on page 115 of this text.

Some abbreviations can go either way: *USA* or *U.S.A.*; *c.o.d.* or *COD*; *r.p.m.* or *rpm*; and so on.

If you don't know whether to use a period or not, check your company's style manual or a good dictionary.

Short Sentences

Sometimes you'll see a period placed after only one word (such as "Yes."), or after a numeral (such as the "3." in the previous section). Why the period? They aren't abbreviations or decimals, and they don't seem to be sentences; they don't have a subject or verb. Well, they are sentences. "Yes.," for example, means, "The answer to your question is 'yes.'" The subject and verb are understood. "3." means, "This is enumeration number 3." Again the subject and verb are understood. For such short sentences, with subject and verb understood, use a period to end them just as with any other sentence.

▶ **A PROOFREADING TIP** ◀

Periods and commas must always be placed INSIDE quotation marks:
Example: "Here, Mrs. Smith," she said. "These are the reports you wanted."

The rule applies even to little quotations:
Example: Rolf received a "C," but Alison earned an "A."

JOB READY? You should be ready to do Job Sheet 17 now!

▼ *Questions and Exclamations (? and !)*

Notice that both the question mark (?) and the exclamation point (!) contain a period. As you know, the period marks a full stop—the end of a sentence. So do the question mark and the exclamation point, and acting as a full stop is the most frequent use of all three marks.

The Question Mark

The **QUESTION MARK** ends a sentence that is a direct question and demands an answer.

Examples:

You went to the store without telling me. Why? ("Why?" here is considered a short sentence. It is understood that it means "Why did you go to the store without telling me?")

What is your name? Where are you from? What do you do for a living? Are you happy? Are there any more at home like you?

These are real questions. But *I asked why you went to the store* is not a question; it's a statement ABOUT a question. Also, some companies use what they call a "polite question," and they don't put a question mark after it, just a period. For example, *"Would you please send your payment at your earliest convenience."* They don't demand an answer; they just demand a payment.

The Exclamation Point

The **EXCLAMATION POINT** ends a sentence which expresses something that would make you want to shout or scream. Exclamation points should not be overused. Just as you stop listening to people who scream too much, you stop paying attention to writing that has too many exclamation points. For example, which of these two versions do you think is the more effective use of exclamation points?

Look! You insulted me last week! You robbed me! You cheated my husband! And now you want to borrow $10,000 from me! No way, Buster!

OR

Look, you insulted me last week, you robbed me, you cheated my husband. And now you want to borrow $10,000 from me? No way, Buster!

Some Other Uses of ? and !

A question mark inside parentheses after a word in a quotation means that whoever is quoting the quote thinks there's something wrong or strange about that word or idea. For example: *Hard work always (?) brings success.*

An exclamation point inside parentheses after a word means that the writer thinks that action or idea is exceptionally good or bad: *Kasparov captured Karpov's king bishop (!) and won.*

56

LET'S TRY!

4-1

Find and correct (with proper proofreader's marks) missing or misplaced periods, question marks, and exclamation points.

0. Hurray/! Did I try hard/? Yes/! And I won∧!

1. At 7 pm∧ I am going to leave for the concert∧
2. The card measured 3 in∧ by 5 in∧ so that it would slip in easily∧
3. The comedian asked why they didn't laugh at his jokes∧
4. The comedian asked, "Why don't you laugh at my jokes?"
5. Yes! The profits last year were fantastic!
6. Would you please send your payment immediately?
7. You went off to Chicago without telling me. Why?
8. John's IQ was 140, but he got only a "C."
9. HI is the two-letter designation for Hawaii.

(Check your work in the Correct Markings *section at the back of this book.)*

(TEMPLATE USERS: Complete this exercise using your template disk.)

Class Exercise 4-1

Directions: Insert missing question marks and exclamation points or delete wrongly placed question marks and exclamation points in the following text. Correct any other punctuation or spelling errors that you find.

```
    Cindy, the last time we talked, you asked, if I could give you any
tips on how to be better organized at the office? Goodness, what an
assignment.  Here is my foolproof patented practical guaranted guide to
absolutely perfect desk organization.
    When the morning mail comes in, do something with every piece right
away.  I bet you think this is impossible?  So did I at first but now I
know it can be done.  I used to let it pile up day after day.  Good
grief, what a collection I had.
    So you look over this kind of mail quickly and toss out everthing
you're sure you'll never have any need for.  That's the easy part, but
what about the memos, letters, reports, etc., that pertain to your daily
work.  Act right away on the ones that need prompt action, and put each
of the others in it's appropriate job folder.  (As you've learned in
English classes, a request stated, "Would you please send me the updated
list of conference attendees immediately," isn't asking for a yes or no
answer; you had better send it immediately—or else.)
    As for those "appropriate" job folders:  I used to keep one folder for
each job, but I've changed that.  Now I keep several folders per job,
each one labeled for a particular category of material (for example,
Membership, Suppliers, Correspondence with Customers).  This method
takes more folders and more storage slots, but, after all, isn't time
more important.
```

(TEMPLATE USERS: Complete this exercise using your template disk.)

Class Exercise 4-2

Directions: Insert missing periods and commas or delete wrongly placed periods and commas using the correct proofreader's marks and the information in Lesson 4. Correct other punctuation and spelling errors in the process.

The morning of Darrell's first job interveiw was rainey, and cold and his hair was a mess when he entered, the big glass office building he rushed to the nearest restroom to do what he could to look better. Already he was five minutes late.

With his hair still damp he finally was told by the receptionist to go on into Ms. Delaney's office Fortunately Ms. Delaney the interviewer was aware of the bad weather and was very understanding about Darrell's appearance.

"Considering the weather, Mr. Smith you did very well to have gotten through the traffic," she said Tell me about your background."

Darrell Smith was gratful, and he proceeded to tell Ms. Delaney that he had just graduated from a business academy recieving a 4.0 average, so that he could learn computer operation. He had previously worked for the F.B.I. and realized that he had to know computers to get along in busyness today.

"Garbage in garbage out," said Ms. Delaney, "You're right, Mr. Smith. When could you start?"

"You mean I can have the job?" asked Darrell.

"Yes, if you'll tell me what a 4.0 average means."

"A."

"That's very good. You've confirmed my judgement, Mr. Smith. Can you start at eight Monday morning?"

"I'll be here at eight sharp," said Darrell.

"Good. Your pay begins at $1,240.50 per month; we look forward to working with you."

Some drops fell onto the edge of the desk. Both Darrell and Ms. Delaney noticed them.

"I'd like to say those are tears of joy, Ms. Delaney, but they're really just raindrops falling from my hair," Darrell said, and he shook hands and left.

(TEMPLATE USERS: Complete this exercise using your template disk.)

Parentheses, Dashes, and Brackets – The Fences

Several different punctuation marks act as fences; that is, these marks enclose information that interrupts the main thought of a sentence. These marks are parentheses, dashes, and brackets.

Parentheses ( ) *deemphasize*

1. You already know that parentheses enclose incidental information and comments that are considered less important than the sentence in which the parentheses appear.
    This necktie (I bought it in Chicago) is my favorite.
2. Parentheses are also used to separate numerals from text.
    He took the following courses: (1) proofreading, (2) computer keyboarding, (3) word processing, and (4) spreadsheets.
3. Parentheses are also used, especially in legal and financial documents, when numbers that have been expressed in words are restated in numerals.
    I owe you three dollars and forty-two cents ($3.42) to be paid on May 5, 1999.

Dashes — *emphasize*

1. Dashes are sometimes used in the place of parentheses to separate comments that interrupt a sentence.
    Dashes—you might say—have a little more dash than parentheses.
2. Dashes are also used to show an interruption or non-completion of a sentence.
    This book is about nouns, pronouns, verbs, punctuation, and—well, you know.
3. Dashes may also set off final explanatory or summarizing words or statements.
    I'll tell you what computer programmers remind me of—geniuses, that's what.
4. Dashes are often used after a quote to tell you who the author is.
    Anybody who goes to see a psychiatrist ought to have his head examined. —Sam Goldwyn
5. Dashes are often used before such words as *namely, for example, that is*, and *for instance*.
    He was talented—for instance, he got "A's" in both chemistry and English.
6. Dashes are sometimes used in place of colons, which will be presented later.
    Here's what we've got to do—sort alphabetically, check the name spellings, and distribute the diplomas in order.

DASHES SHOULD NOT BE OVERUSED. THEY MAKE TEXT DIFFICULT TO READ.

60

Brackets [ ]

Brackets will not be much of a problem for proofreaders. Editors, not proofreaders, use brackets to enclose comments or clarifications to sentences that someone else wrote. Proofreaders are not supposed to change the meaning of what others write. If they are proofreading their own writing, they use parentheses, not brackets, when they want to add comments or clarifications. About the only time proofreaders concern themselves about brackets is when the text they are reading already has brackets. Then all they have to do is make sure that the brackets enclose something that comments on or clarifies something in the sentence but is not at all a part of the sentence. Here are some correct uses of brackets to give you an idea of what they do.

1. Brackets are used to insert into a sentence something that is important to the meaning of the basic sentence, such as a clarification made by an editor:
   This really is the signature of [Benjamin] Franklin.
2. Brackets are also used to insert parenthetical information into a passage that is already inside parentheses:
   (They made more corrections in the fifth [1990] edition than in any other.)
3. Brackets are used to insert words omitted in a quotation:
   "At the end of the play, both [Romeo and Juliet] die."
4. Brackets are used to insert "sic," the Latin word that means "thus" (or, "That's what the writer said, not what I said.") For example, a scholar writes what a famous author once wrote, and adds "sic" to show he, the scholar, didn't misquote:
   "Hitler was not [sic] evil."

> **LET'S TRY!**   4-2

Find and correct with proper proofreader's marks missing or misplaced parentheses, dashes, and brackets.

0. Patricia (I always did like her) sent in the best essay — the third to come in.

1. I promise to pay the sum of fourteen dollars and twelve cents ($14.12) on or before March 15, 1995.

2. The rules of the game (I found them in the attic) are to be followed precisely.

3. I think — no, I know — we should acquire that company.

4. There's only one thing to do — accept their terms.

5. When they walked off the plane (what a dishevelled group they were — wrinkled and drooping with fatigue) Sebastian popped open a bottle of champagne [imported] for them.

(Check your work in the **Correct Markings** *section at the back of this book.)*

 (TEMPLATE USERS: Complete this exercise using your template disk.)

JOB READY?   You should be ready to do Job Sheets 18* and 19 now!

Colons – The Announcers

A colon in a sentence says essentially, "Something important or specific is coming up next in this sentence."

Examples:

Please bring the following: pencil, paper, and a dictionary.
Pamela Jones wrote three books: THE BEGINNING, THE MIDDLE, and THE END.
Donna had only one criticism of Barb: she wasn't assertive enough.
Here are some examples of stupidity: (students fill in here).

NOTE: Here's what happens when you substitute a dash for the colon:
Donna had only one criticism of Barb—she wasn't assertive enough.

Do you see that the dash makes it more emphatic, less formal, and not very subtle? But remember, dashes should not be overused. They make text difficult to read.

Other Uses of the Colon

1. The colon is still used after the salutation in a formal letter and in many business letters, even though the modern style is to use no punctuation after salutations or complimentary closes of business letters.

Examples:

Dear Senator Domenici: Dear Sir: Dear Madame:

2. The colon is used between hours and minutes *(11:45 a.m.)*.
3. The colon is used between chapter and verse in scriptural passages *(Matt. 10:5-9)*.
4. The colon is used between volume and page numbers *(The Dallas News, Vol. III:17)*.

Let's Try!

4-3

Find and correct, with proper proofreader's marks, missing or misplaced colons.

0. You should know three things⁁reading, writing, and arithmetic.

1. When you use closed punctuation in a business letter, your salutation should read, "Dear _____" and "Sincerely yours," is the way your complimentary close should read.

2. There are four steps in writing a sales letter (1) gain attention, (2) create interest, (3) develop desire, and (4) get action.

3. My grandmother's favorite Bible passage was Matthew 10 5.

4. I'll meet you at 2.15 this afternoon.

5. This would be Vol. II 10 of the newsletter.

(Check your work in the Correct Markings *section at the back of this book.)*

(TEMPLATE USERS: Complete this exercise using your template disk.)

Class Exercise 4-3

Directions: Insert missing parentheses, colons, and dashes, or delete wrongly placed parentheses, brackets, colons, and dashes in the following text, using information provided in Lesson 4 thus far. Correct any spelling errors found in the process, using the proper proofreader's marks.

MEMORANDUM

TO: Bradley Thomas, Buyer
FROM: Cathryn H. Atwater, Manager
DATE: November 5, 19--
SUBJECT: SPRING BUYING TRIP

Please make plans to depart on your 1st buying trip for our 1994 spring merchandise immediately after our Thanksgiveing promotion. (yes, I realize we haven't obtained all our 1993 Christmas stock yet).

The reason we must begin thinking of spring now is simply that we recall only too well the unconscionable shortages we experienced this last spring. We now have analyses that show we lost at least $700,000 in sales last spring because of shortages of merchandise you know, having to tell customers, "Sorry, we're out of stock." That means we lost about $35,000 in net profit, just about the amount of yhur base salary, incidentally.

Getting this early start on the spring buying trip should not interfere with your well-planned last-minute [Christmas] buying trip. I am sure that most of the conventions and manufacturers shows you plans to attend will be excellent sources of information about the expected features of spring lines in addition to promotion of the the lastest potential high mark-up items for Christmas sales.

On this double-duty trip we want you to do an in-depth analysis of the markets in the following centers: Dallas, Chicago, New York, and San Francisco. Depending upon your findings, you are authorized to commit up to $300,000 over and above your existing Christmas budget. Please as usual submit daily FAX reports on your progress. Oh yes, and good luck!

(TEMPLATE USERS: Complete this exercise using your template disk.)

JOB READY? You should be ready to do Job Sheet 20* now!

The Double Consonant Spelling Rule

The rule for doubling consonants when you add a suffix to a word that ends in a consonant has three parts.

1. If you have a ONE-SYLLABLE word that ends in a *consonant* preceded by a single *vowel* (such as *run*), double that final consonant before adding a suffix that begins with a *vowel*.

Examples:

run + ing becomes *running*,   *sit + ing* becomes *sitting*, *pop + ing* becomes *popping*.

2. If a word ends in a *consonant* preceded by a *vowel*, and if it has MORE THAN ONE SYLLABLE, you double the final consonant when adding a suffix ONLY if the word is accented on the final syllable. *Notice that this is really the same as the first part of the rule, because a one-syllable word, by definition, has its accent on the final syllable. There's only one syllable; therefore it has to be the accented one.*

Examples:

begin + ing becomes *beginning*   *admit + ance* becomes *admittance*.

3. If the word ends in a *consonant* preceded by a *vowel* and has MORE THAN ONE SYLLABLE, but its accent is not on the final syllable, you do not double the final consonant.

Examples:

credit + ing becomes *crediting*   *elicit + ing* becomes *eliciting*
differ + ent becomes *different*   *credit + able* becomes *creditable*.

LET'S TRY!

4-4

Find and correct, with proper proofreader's marks, the words that disobey the Double Consonant Spelling Rule.

0. In accounting, I always had trouble crediting and debiting correctly, but I was always good at wining money at beting.

    The administrative assistant was baring the door when Wolfgang tried to gain admitance to the director's office. "Stop beging me to get in," she said. "None of your clever maneuverring will do any good. You certainly won't be eliciting any positive responses from me!" Wolfgang, however, was merely fulfiling his promise to the director not to leave without visiting him once more. Wolfgang was begining to get angry. He could see that yelling would do no good; there were obviously grave differrences in their interprettations of the situation. So he decided to be personnable. He smiled charmingly and said, "Look, I wasn't kiding; he really wants to see me. You could be buzing him to find out. Would you do that?" Still glowerring, she picked up the phone. She learned that Wolfgang was right. Reluctantly, she decided that leting him in was the thing to do. She had no rebutal.

(Check your work in the Correct Markings *section at the back of this book.)*

(TEMPLATE USERS: Complete this exercise using your template disk.)

JOB READY? You should be ready to do Job Sheet 21 now!

Lesson 5

Proofreading for Apostrophes, Quotations, Asterisks, Ellipses, Hyphens, Slashes, Spelling

When you complete this Lesson, you will be able to achieve the following objectives:

▶ **Objective Number 22:** Proofread, using the correct proofreader's marks, text containing errors in the use of apostrophes that show possession, show omission, and that are used as sub-quotation marks; and contain errors in the use of possessive pronouns. Performance standard: 90 percent.

▶ **Objective Number 23:** Proofread, using the correct proofreader's marks, text containing errors in uses of single and double quotation marks in multi-paragraph quotations. Performance standard: 100 percent.

▶ **Objective Number 24:** Proofread, using the correct proofreader's marks, text containing errors in the use of asterisks and ellipses. Performance standard: 100 percent.

▶ **Objective Number 25:** Proofread, using the correct proofreader's marks, text containing errors in the use of hyphens and slashes (virgules). Performance standard: 100 percent.

▶ **Objective Number 26*:** Proofread, using the correct proofreader's marks, text containing a random selection of grammatical, punctuation, and spelling errors. Performance standard: 100 percent.

▶ **Objective Number 27:** Spell correctly at least 80 percent of an orally given list of words that involve use of the following three spelling rules: the Final CE/GE Spelling Rule, the Final OE Spelling Rule, and the DIS/MIS/UN/AS/IL/IR Prefix Rule.

Punctuation III

In this Lesson you will learn the uses of additional punctuation marks. Each mark has a different set of messages. For example, an **apostrophe (')** signals either that the person, place, or thing denoted by the word it's used in possesses something, or that some letters have been left out of the word. A set of **quotation marks (")** signals that some person or piece of writing is being directly quoted. An **asterisk (*)** signals either that the writer is calling attention to a word or group of words that he or she is going to say more about in a footnote at the bottom of the page, or, if it is combined with other asterisks, that a period of time has gone by. The **ellipsis dots (. . .)** signal that something in a quotation has been left out, or (usually in fiction) that a speaker is hesitating. The **hyphen (-)** signals either that a word has been broken into two parts so it will not run into the margin, or that two or more words are being combined into the equivalent of one word. And, finally, the **slash (/)**, which is also called a "virgule" by people who like to use unusual words, signals that the writer is trying to save space by avoiding writing the words "or" or "per," or is separating two or more parts of a single concept.

Let's look at each one of these punctuation marks in more detail so that we can catch errors in their uses as we proofread.

Apostrophes — What Do They Do?

The apostrophe (') is used to show ownership or possession of a person, place, thing, or idea. It is also used to signal that some letter or letters have been omitted from a word.

Apostrophes Show Possession

To show that a *singular* noun or a plural noun that does not end in *s* is the possessor of (owns) something, add an apostrophe and an *s* to that noun.

Examples:

    a child's plaything   Charles's aunt   children's toys

To show that a *plural* noun ending in *s* is the possessor of (owns) something, add the apostrophe after that final *s*.

Examples:

    the ladies' gowns   the officers' troops   the stores' sales

To show that a *singular* noun that ends in *s* or *x* or *z* is the possessor of (owns) something, you have two choices: (a) if it would sound ridiculous to add another "es" sound when you pronounce it, simply add the apostrophe after the word.

Examples:
   Moses' Law (Pronounced "Mosezez Law," it sounds silly.)
   For righteousness' sake ("righteousnessez" also sounds silly.)

   (b) if it sounds OK to add another "es" sound when you pronounce it, then add either just an apostrophe or an apostrophe plus *s*.

Examples:
   Mr. Gomez' store or Mr. Gomez's [Gomezez] store.
   Mr. Jones' car or Mr. Jones's [Jonzez] car.
   Knox' gelatine or Knox's [Noxez] gelatine.

To show that an indefinite pronoun is the possessor of (owns) something, you add an apostrophe and an *s* just as you do with a singular noun.

Examples:
   everyone's cat   one's motorbike   everybody's friend

To show that a hyphenated compound word, a multi-name business firm, or a word showing joint possession is the possessor of (owns) something, you add an apostrophe and an *s* to the last word only.

Examples:
   mother-in-law's house   Shearson-Lehman's profits

▶ LET'S TRY!   5-1

Find and correct mistakes in the use of apostrophes showing possession.

0. Willis' computer's keyboard keys make loud clicks.

1. The women's movement has brought about many changes.

2. The pickup truck's headlights were set too high.

3. Phylisses' husband was a telemarketing supervisor.

4. There was no place to check the ladies' purses.

5. Food was better at the enlisted men's and women's mess than at the officers' mess.

6. Everyone's car should be checked for emissions.

7. The stray cat is not Mary's, Guss's, Jill's, or anyone else's.

(Check your work in the **Correct Markings** *section at the back of this book.*)

💾 (TEMPLATE USERS: Complete this exercise using your template disk.)

71

Apostrophes Can Show Omission

To show that a letter or letters are left out of a word, substitute an apostrophe. This use of an apostrophe gives us all the familiar contractions you know, such as *I'll, didn't, don't, I've, you're, we're, I'm, you'd*, and so on. It also gives us such shortened forms as *o'clock* (of the clock), *jack-o'-lantern* (Jack of the Lantern), *cont'd* (continued), and so on.

To show the omission of the century in a date, substitute an apostrophe.

Examples:

She was a hippie during the '60s.   He served from '78 to '83.

To show the plural of a single figure, letter, or symbol, use an apostrophe.

Examples:

Watch *p*'s and *q*'s.   Dot your *i*'s.   Use *&*'s rarely.   Know the *ABC*'s.

Let's Try!   5-2

Find and correct mistakes in the use of apostrophes showing omission.

0. Haven't you learned the proofreader's marks? You'd better.

1. Didn't he tell you I'm going to be here?

2. We're happy to be out of the '60s era.

3. They've been at 6's and 7's all their lives. They're always at cross purposes.

4. You're going to get your comeuppance someday.

5. George said to arrive by six o'clock.

(Check your work in the **Correct Markings** *section at the back of this book.)*

(TEMPLATE USERS: Complete this exercise using your template disk.)

> **A PROOFREADING TIP** <

The personal pronouns **its, ours, yours, theirs, whose, hers** are already possessive. They don't need an apostrophe.

POSSESSIVES	CONTRACTIONS
its = belongs to it	it's = it is
ours = belongs to us	(*there is no our's*)
yours = belongs to you	(*there is no your's*)
your = belonging to you	you're = you are
theirs = belongs to them	(*there is no their's*)
their = belonging to them	they're = they are
whose = belonging to "who"	who's = who is
hers = belongs to her	(*there is no her's*)

Don't insert apostrophes into possessive personal pronouns!

▶ LET'S TRY!

5-3

Find and correct mistakes in the use of apostrophes with personal and possessive pronouns.

0. It's not yours and it's not hers. I don't know whose it is.

1. Its its own trademark.

2. I don't know whose going, nor whose car this is.

3. These groceries are ours, those are yours, and those others are theirs.

4. Its not going to be easy.

5. Where did it get its name?

(*Check your work in the* Correct Markings *section at the back of this book.*)

(TEMPLATE USERS: Complete this exercise using your template disk.)

Quotation Marks—What Do They Do?

Quotation marks are used in a variety of ways. They can be used to show the exact words someone says, writes, or thinks, or they can be used to emphasize a word or highlight a title. Six uses of quotation marks are described in the following sections.

1. Enclosing Direct Quotations

"Enclose" means that a set of quotation marks (") appears at the beginning of a direct quote, and it must be balanced by another quotation mark (") at the end of the direct quote. A good proofreader always checks to see that a quotation mark at the beginning is balanced by one at the end.

A direct quotation consists of the exact words someone said or wrote. If the sentence says something such as *Kate said that Jessica will win the race*, it is not giving a direct quotation. Nothing is being quoted; the sentence is merely giving an approximation of what Kate said. But if the sentence says *Kate said, "Jessica will win the race,"* then the sentence is saying exactly what Kate said. It is quoting her; therefore, you have a direct quotation that must be enclosed by quotation marks. Good proofreaders look for *"that"* in such a sentence, and if they don't find it, it is likely that there should be some quotation marks in the sentence.

"Go home," she said. That's a sentence with a direct quotation. Note that the quotation begins with a capital letter. The quotation is a full sentence. All quoted full sentences begin with a capital letter. But if the quote is not a full sentence, the quoted material does not begin with a capital letter. For example: *According to him, the book is "a definitive study."*

And don't forget what you learned in Lesson 3, "Commas separate direct quotations from the rest of the sentence." Use commas before and after if the quotation is in the middle of the sentence.

2. Enclosing Words That Define a Noun

When a new or foreign word is being defined in a sentence, that new or foreign word should be enclosed in quotation marks.

Example:

The word "toro" is Spanish for bull.

3. Enclosing Exact Thoughts

Remember, the only thoughts that get enclosed within quotation marks are exact thoughts. You treat exact thoughts just as if they'd been said aloud.

Example:

"This place is a zoo!" he thought.

4. Enclosing Certain Titles

Enclose the titles of TV programs, magazine articles, songs, short stories, essays, and poems in quotation marks.

Examples:

"Star Trek"   "How To Lose Weight" in *Health Today*
The song, "Yesterday"
"Ode on a Grecian Urn," by Keats
"Self-Reliance," by Ralph Waldo Emerson

LET'S TRY! 5-4

Find and correct mistakes in the use of quotation marks.

0. He never said that ⟨"⟩he couldn't do it.⟨"⟩ He always said, "I can."

1. The tennis coach said that ⟨"⟩Arturo is sure to win the match.⟨"⟩

2. The tennis coach's actual words were, "Arturo is sure to win the match."

3. She said, "I hope you have a nice trip," and then she cried.

4. The word "tia" is Spanish for aunt.

5. He tried to recall his actual thoughts. Yes, they were, "Why did I put down my briefcase before knocking on the door?"

6. The only program he watched on CBS was "60 Minutes."

(Check your work in the **Correct Markings** *section at the back of this book.)*

(TEMPLATE USERS: Complete this exercise using your template disk.)

5. The "Sub-Quote" or "Single Quote"

Suppose you come across a passage being quoted, and you find another quoted passage inside the original quotation such as in the following:

The author said, "When I begin writing, I always say to myself, 'Don't quit until you've written at least three pages,' and then I start."

or this:

The author said, "When I begin writing, I always read the article, 'How To Write,' and then I start."

See what was done? A regular set of (double) quotation marks (") was put at the beginning of what the author said, and (in the first example above) a single quotation mark (') was put at the beginning and end of what the author said to himself. Or, (in the second example above) it was put at the beginning and end of the name of the article.

The single mark is best called a *sub-quote* or a *single quote*. To make it, you use a single quotation mark—similar to an apostrophe—rather than a regular double quotation mark. The difference between " and ' helps the reader keep track of which quote is the main quote, and which is a quote within a quote. When proofreading, if you must insert a single quote (sub-quote), you do it in exactly the same way you insert an apostrophe — this way:

JOB READY?   You should be ready to do Job Sheet 22 now!

6. Special Rules for Multi-Paragraph Quotations

When quotations are more than a paragraph long, begin each new paragraph with a quotation mark, but omit the quotation mark at the end of each paragraph, except the last paragraph. Note the quotation marks in the following:

The book said: "English teachers make the study of English grammar much more difficult than it really is.

"There is a lot more consistency in the rules than it seems, simply because each teacher is more interested in showing how many fancy words he or she knows than in helping students understand the consistency of this great language.

"So teachers should learn to be proud of making the study of language simpler, not more complex."

Now, if you can find and correct errors with both single and double quotes in a multi-paragraph quotation, you are indeed a good proofreader!

JOB READY?   You should be ready to do Job Sheet 23 now!

LET'S TRY!

5-5

Find and correct mistakes in the use of double and single quotation marks in multi-paragraph quotations.

0. Mom said, "Yes, I know they say, 'Too many cooks spoil the broth.' But there's another proverb I like better:
"'Many hands make light work.' And with that she turned off the TV, grabbed me by the collar, and marched me into the kitchen.

When my grandfather was in his eighties, he came to live with Dad and Mom and me. He was fun to talk to, and I spent a lot of time with him.

"Gramp," I said one day, "tell me about your first job after college."

"Well, I felt pretty lucky to get a job," he said. "Jobs were hard to find in those days, and when they said, 'You're hired—report for work Monday morning at eight,' I couldn't believe my ears."
"I felt like a big shot reporting for work in the brand-new suit the folks had bought me when I graduated. When the supervisor saw me, his jaw dropped. 'What's that getup you're wearing?' he asked. 'You'll wear overalls like everybody else on the shop floor.'

"Remember, Todd, I had my engineering degree by then. But I learned in a hurry that an engineer just starting out had to show that he knew how to clean and fix a machine before he'd be given a job designing one. It wasn't what I hoped to spend my whole life doing, but I'd grown up hearing my parents say, 'All work is noble.' It drove me crazy to hear that quoted over and over again when I was a kid, and I groused about having to spend Saturday morning cleaning the garage or polishing the car, but it's been pretty helpful at times."

(Check your work in the Correct Markings section at the back of this book.)

(TEMPLATE USERS: Complete this exercise using your template disk.)

Asterisks and Ellipses

Asterisks (*) are used to mark unnumbered footnotes, and sometimes to indicate the passage of time in a story. The word "asterisk" comes from Greek, and means "little star." The following example shows how the asterisk is placed when it is used in text as an indication of a footnote.

Example:

The pilot kept looking at the airline chart* and, as a result, she found her way.

Then, at the bottom (or foot) of the page will be another asterisk in front of the footnote itself. A line an inch or so long will separate the text from the footnote in this manner:

Example: _____
*"Chart" is the word airlines use for their maps.

It's all right to use asterisks for footnotes if there are only one or two in a document. Two asterisks (**) are used for the second footnote on a page. But when a document has many footnotes, superior numbers (small numbers printed above the line) should be used instead of asterisks.

To show passage of time, three asterisks (* * *) are sometimes used between lines.

Ellipsis Dots (. . .) show the omission of words in a story or a quotation, an unfinished thought, or an abrupt change of thought. Ellipses always come in threes:

". . . government of the people, . . . and for the people."

The first ellipses show that all the first part of Lincoln's Gettysburg Address has been left out. The second ellipses show that something else ("by the people,") has been left out. Notice that the correct comma after the first "people" is added to the dots. If something were left out at the end of the sentence, there would be four dots — three ellipsis dots and one period.

78

LET'S TRY! 5-6

Find and correct mistakes in the use of asterisks and ellipses.

0. An asterisk looks like this: (*). An ellipsis looks like this: (...).

1. The word "molybdenum"* is difficult to pronounce.

2. As a young lad he lived on a farm where his life consisted mostly of hiking, climbing trees, and taking care of animals.

   * * *

   Twenty years later, he was still hiking, climbing trees, and taking care of animals. He worked in a zoo.

3. "Mary had a little lamb... And everywhere that Mary went, the lamb was sure to go."

---
*"Molybdenum" is a metallic element used chiefly to make a hard steel alloy.

(Check your work in the Correct Markings section at the back of this book.)

(TEMPLATE USERS: Complete this exercise using your template disk.)

79

Class Exercise 5-1

Directions: Proofread and correct the following text containing errors in the use of apostrophes, quotation marks, ellipses, asterisks, and spelling.

Doris* said she had a funny experience when she was being interviewed for her first job. The interviewer had gone over her resume with her, talked about her school record, told her something about the job duties, and then asked out of the blue, "do you know how to use the telephone."

Doris was'nt prepared for such a question and finaly stammered, "Why, yes, uh . . . of course, uh * * * Ive been using the telephone all my life, I guess youd say'.

Silence came from the interviewer who just stared at Dorises face, waiting for her to go on. Well, you pick up the recievner and say hello or good morning and the name of the company, and. . .

More silence. More staring. Feeling desperate, Doris said, Its pretty important, I guess, because the callers going to get a good or bad impression of the company from the way it's employees sound when they answer the phone. I alwayss think it's rude when the person on the other end says, Whose calling? or Hold on. Should'nt there be a Please or a Thank you put in somewhere?

Also, I feel a little hurt if the person answering just says, hes not in. That makes me think he really is in, but just doesn't wa'nt to hear from me. And I absolutely hate it when the other person slams down the receiver. Ouch!

The interviewer grinned. "Good work!" he said. We may have a spot for you."

_____

*Not her real name

(TEMPLATE USERS: Complete this exercise using your template disk.)

JOB READY? You should be ready to do Job Sheet 24 now!

Hyphens—How To Use Them

Hyphens divide words that are too long to fit on a line of type, and they link words so that the separate words act as one word. The only problems with hyphens are (1) where to use them to make a break, and (2) which words should be linked with hyphens and which should not.

End-of-Line Hyphens

The most frequent use of a hyphen is to divide a word at the end of a line. If you know how to use a dictionary, and if you know a few simple rules about line breaks, you should never have a problem correcting mistakes in hyphenation at the end of a line.

USE THE DICTIONARY! A typical dictionary entry looks something like this:

mo•lyb'•de•num

The dots separate what are called *syllables*. A syllable is one or more letters that make a single, separate sound in a word. End-of-line words may be divided by hyphens only between syllables. So, now you know where the hyphens could go in the word "molybdenum".

mo-lybdenum   *molyb-denum*   *molybde-num*

Notice that the hyphen follows the vowel and precedes the consonant twice in this word: *mo-lybdenum* and *molybde-num*. That's pretty normal for most words, so, in general, you can use that rule and save looking up the word in the dictionary. But, if you're in doubt, remember that THE DICTIONARY is the authority. Notice also that the other hyphen is between two consonants (*y* here is counted as a vowel); that's also a pretty normal occurrence, so, again, you can save looking-up time.

If the copy you are proofreading breaks *molybdenum* in any one of the three possible places, you won't have to make any corrections. The most widely followed rule for dividing words at the end of a line is:

Never a syllable with fewer than two letters at the end of a line, and never fewer than three letters at the beginning of the next line.

Obviously, you can't break a word with only one syllable.

Here are a few more rules for breaking words at the end of a line:

1. It's okay to put a hyphen before *ing* or *able* or *ible* at the end of a line. For example: *learn-ing   understand-able   leg-ible*
2. BUT if the *ing* is preceded by a double consonant (as in *running, dubbing, mugging*), hyphenate between the double letters and carry over the one consonant to the next line. For example: *run-ning   dub-bing   mug-ging*.
3. A person's surname (family name) or given name should never be broken up by a hyphen. Don't allow: *John-son   Andrei-vitch   Eliza-beth*.

81

4. Abbreviations with numerals should never be separated from the numerals. For example: *For 1,000 mi.,* never allow *1,000-mi. For A.D. 1492,* never allow *A.D.-1492.* For *11:50 a.m.,* never allow *11:50-a.m.*
5. Some words are always hyphenated (more about that later)—words such as *self-determination* or *able-bodied.* If such a word occurs at the end of a line, be sure it is hyphenated where it is normally hyphenated and not somewhere else. For example, *self-determination* not *self-determination.*
6. Words with well-known prefixes should be hyphenated at the end of that prefix, if the word comes at the end of a line. For example: Divide the word *disinterested* after the *dis,* in this manner: *dis-interested* Don't allow it to be hyphenated anywhere else.
7. Don't allow breaks in words that would possibly confuse readers after the word is broken. For example, *of-ten* would put an *of* at the end of one line and a *ten* at the beginning of the next.

As you read these rules, notice that they are really just common sense. And, remember:

WHEN IN DOUBT, USE THE DICTIONARY.

Words That Must Be Hyphenated

Not all hyphens occur at the end of a line. Some combinations of words must be joined by hyphens to make the equivalent of one word, no matter where they occur in text. General rules for these follow.

1. All "in-laws" must be hyphenated. You know these: *mother-in-law father-in-law brother-in-law sister-in-law.* Yes, and *attorney-at-law.*
2. When someone has been elected to office but hasn't started his or her job yet, the title must be hyphenated: *President-elect   senator-elect   chairman-elect.*
3. Spelled-out fractions must be hyphenated: *five-eighths   two-thirds   one-half   fifteen-sixteenths   three-quarters.*
4. Compounds of the word "great" used with relatives must be hyphenated: *great-grandmother   great-aunt   great-uncle*
5. Compounds with the word "vice" may be hyphenated: *vice-president vice-chairman   vice-director*   But not "vice squad." Those are two separate words and a different meaning of "vice."
6. All compounds beginning with the word "self" are hyphenated: *self-assured   self-hate   self-confident   self-conscious   self-taught   self-indulgent*
7. When a group of words is used as an adjective that precedes the noun, it should be hyphenated. But when the group FOLLOWS the noun, it should not be hyphenated. You'll get the idea from these examples:

    up-to-date figures   BUT   The figures were up to date.
    matter-of-fact writing   BUT   The writing was matter of fact.
    a how-to-do-it book   BUT   The book tells how to do it.
8. Verb-adverb compounds that act as nouns, such as *the go-ahead* and *the run-around,* as in *He gave her the go-ahead, but she gave him the run-around,* should be hyphenated.

9. Compounds with the word "all" should nearly always be hyphenated before the word that "all" describes: *all-out   all-time all-powerful all-American*   (The combination *all told* is an exception; don't hyphenate it.)
10. Many compound words are made up of some noun plus *like* as a suffix. Most often no hyphen is necessary with them (except at the end of a line) because they are written as one word, such as: *childlike, catlike, booklike,* etc. But if the noun ends in the letter "l," (as in *fall,* for example), it would look silly to make it one word— you'd have three "l's" together—so you use a hyphen. Then you have *fall-like,* instead of *falllike.* Also use a hyphen if the noun is a proper noun (*California-like, Lincoln-like,* and so on.)

As a proofreader, you will encounter most hyphenation errors among words that must be hyphenated when writers violate Rule 7. Review that rule carefully. Remember that an *adjective* is a word that describes, alters, adds to, or otherwise specifies the meaning of a *noun*. If two or more words work together to describe a noun, then those words act as a single adjective. A hyphen must connect them to show that they work together as an adjective. That's your up-to-the-minute information.

LET'S TRY!

5-7

Find and correct mistakes in the use of hyphens.

0. You can hyphenate the word "involvement" in one of two places: after the "n" in "in," or before the "m" in "ment." In other words, you could hyphenate like this: *involvement*, or *involvement*.

1. Although he seemed self-assured, he was really filled with self doubt.

2. Although almost three quarters of the earth is covered with water, 100 percent of the people on earth live on the land.

3. The new edition of the book has been brought completely up to date.

4. The up-to-date edition of the book is just off the presses.

5. All told, the all time all Americans are few.

6. She gave them the go ahead, but they gave her the run-around.

7. His great aunt was really great.

8. One thing about her was that she was full of self-determination.

9. My mother in law became president elect of the club.

(Check your work in the Correct Markings section at the back of this book.)

(TEMPLATE USERS: Complete this exercise using your template disk.)

Slashes (Virgules) — What Do They Do? (/)

The grammarian's name for the SLASH is the "virgule." But many people call it the "slash." You can call it "virgule" if you want to, but hardly anyone outside of your class will know what you're talking about.

The SLASH has several important correct uses:

1. The expression "and/or" as in *boys and/or girls,* may mean "just boys," "just girls," or "both boys and girls."
2. The slash also is used in the informal statement of dates, such as *10/27/93* for October 27, 1993.
3. The slash is used to abbreviate "in care of" as in *c/o*.
4. The slash substitutes for the word "per" in abbreviated statements of rate, as in: *The interstate speed limit is 65 miles/hour. No consultant should work for less than $30/hour. Room rates at that hotel begin at $100/day.*

JOB READY?   You should be ready to do Job Sheet 25 now!

Class Exercise 5-2

Directions: Correct missing or wrongly placed apostrophes, quotation marks, asterisks, ellipses, hyphens, and slashes in the following text. Some misspellings must also be corrected.

Over the past few months, I've heard some of you worry out loud that, "your afraid we're getting too busy to catch all the errors in the written correspondence we send out." Well, I didnt think to much about it until the other day when a memo I'd sent to Jack Davis in Human Resources came back with two mispellings circled and "tsk, tsk" written in the margin. Now, Jacks an old friend of mine and likes to kid around, but when I saw him later in the cafeteria and he told me that "I didn't seem to be keeping an eye on quality in my department any more," I began to get worried too. Its high time I did a little self-examination, I said to myself, after all, the errors Jack marked were my errors, not anybody elses.

So, though this may look like just one more bosses memo to his staff (ho hum, heres another one, its really the boss giving himself a talking-to. (After all Ive had many more years experience proofreading than you have and ought to do better). These are the things I'm reminding myself:

1. No matter how rushed you feel, take time to do what my first boss said so often it sounded like a foot-ball cheer: "look it up. Check it out. Read it over.

2. You think your a great speller, dont you. Well, you still need a dictionery. Is it "-ible" or "-able?" Is it "-ence" or "-ance"? Look it up.

3. If something looks fishy, a name spelled two different ways or a bunch of numbers that dont add up, ask the person who wrote it. Dont guess; check it out.

3. After youve read it word for word, stand back a bit and run your eye over each page again. Are paragraph indents consistent? Are end-of-line word breaks checked? Are numbered or lettered sequences OK? "Of course they are," you say? It's impossible to make that kind of error? Hmm-.

(TEMPLATE USERS: Complete this exercise using your template disk.)

JOB READY? You should be ready to do Job Sheet 26* now!

Three Spelling Rules: The FINAL CE/GE Spelling Rule; The FINAL OE Spelling Rule; The DIS/MIS/UN/AS/IL/IR Prefix Rule

If you learn the three spelling rules below, you'll be able to spell correctly many frequently misspelled words.

1. The FINAL CE/GE Spelling Rule

If you have a word that ends in *ce* or *ge*, keep the final *e* if the suffix you want to add is *ous* or *able*.

Examples:

embrace + *able* becomes *embraceable*; *manage* + *able* becomes *manageable*; *advantage* + *ous* becomes *advantageous*; *knowledge* + *able* becomes *knowledgeable*.

2. The FINAL OE Spelling Rule

If you have a word that ends in *oe*, keep the final *e* when adding a suffix.

Examples:

shoe + *ing* becomes *shoeing*; *hoe* + *ing* becomes *hoeing*.

3. The DIS/MIS/UN/AS/IL/IR Prefix Rule

If you add the prefix *dis, mis, un, as, il,* or *ir* to a root word that begins with the same letter as the final letter of the prefix (that's *s, n, l,* or *r* in these cases), you should double the letters.

Examples:

dis + *service* = *disservice*; *mis* + *spell* = *misspell*; *un* + *necessary* = *unnecessary*; *as* + *sumption* = *assumption*; *il* + *logical* = *illogical*; *ir* + *rational* = *irrational*.

▶ LET'S TRY! 5-8

Find and correct mistakes in the spelling of words that follow the Final CE/GE, the Final OE, and DIS/MIS/UN/AS/IL/IR Prefix Spelling Rules.

0. *(Example)* The worst word to mi̭spell is "misspell."

It takes good managment to spell every word correctly, but when a company does so, it finds the practice very advantagous, because it shows that the company is knowledgable. There's a horseshoing business out West that mispells words all the time, and instead of being couragous enough to hire someone to teach their horseshors how to spell, the owners mispend their money on ilicit, ilogical, and irational projects. It's really outragous what they do. They are truely iresponsible.

(Check your work in the Correct Markings *section at the back of this book.)*

(TEMPLATE USERS: Complete this exercise using your template disk.)

JOB READY? You should be ready to do Job Sheet 27 now!

Lesson 6

Editing: Wordiness, Redundancy, Outdated or Overused Expressions, Clichés, Precision, Logic

When you complete this Lesson, you will be able to achieve the following objectives:

▶ ***Objective Number 28*:*** Proofread and edit, using the correct proofreader's marks, text containing errors of excessive wordiness and redundancy, with 100 percent accuracy of proofreader's marks and 90 percent completeness of editing.

▶ ***Objective Number 29*:*** Proofread and edit, using the correct proofreader's marks, text containing errors in the use of clichés, hackneyed expressions, unnecessary foreign terms, misspellings, and wordy sentences. Performance standard: 100 percent accuracy of proofreader's marks and 90 percent on completeness of editing.

▶ ***Objective Number 30*:*** Proofread and edit, using the correct proofreader's marks, text written in illogical sequence and containing misspellings and excessive use of the passive voice, with 100 percent accuracy of proofreader's marks and 90 percent completeness of editing.

Editing

In this Lesson, you will get an idea of some of the basic things that people called EDITORS do. Here is the real difference between an *editor* and a *proofreader*. A proofreader makes sure that all the individual words and sentences are grammatically correct, all punctuation is correct, and all spelling is correct. An editor is more concerned with whether the writing conveys the meaning that the writer intended to convey, whether the sequence of ideas is logical, whether the words used are appropriate, whether there are too many words, and how to change the writing to make it better.

Editors must get rid of wordiness, clichés, and hackneyed expressions, as one part of their work. They must also get rid of the passive voice as much as possible. They must put phrases, clauses, sentences, paragraphs, and sometimes whole chapters into a more logical sequence. They must make nouns and verbs stronger and more vivid.

Editors do much more, but they have to know how to do those things before they can do more—and everything else they learn on the job.

An editor uses the same proofreader's marks that a proofreader does, but the changes an editor makes are usually bigger. An editor can take over a proofreader's job rather easily, but a proofreader must usually work many years before being promoted into an editing position.

You have probably already noticed from reading the beginning of this Lesson that your objectives will be to edit copy for wordiness, clichés, hackneyed expressions, logical sequence, avoidance of passive voice, and the other things that make ordinary writing better. The information you need for achieving these objectives begins on the next page.

Editing is fun. Few activities are more satisfying than making an otherwise tame or ordinary piece of writing become—all because of your editing—a piece of writing that seems to sing.

An Editor's Questions

Editors have to ask and answer several questions when they are going over a manuscript. The overriding questions are: Is it accurate? Is it clear? Is it logical? Is it concise? Does it overuse the passive voice?

Is It Accurate?

There are three ways to be accurate. You have to be **complete, correct,** and **consistent.**

To be **COMPLETE** you must do everything you can to be certain that nothing is left out of whatever it is you are editing. You double-check all times, names, addresses, dates, and the like by careful rereading. You compare what you are reading with the rough draft, if there is one, or by asking the original writer about any questions that come to your mind. If what you are reading has columns of figures or data, you use a ruler or a card to be sure the columns line up and that all the information is there. Mostly, you go at your job with the assumption that somehow something has been left out of what you're reading.

For example, suppose you were editing an announcement of a meeting, and the copy you were reading said:

> *On Tuesday you'll have your choice of seven exciting seminars to attend: Selling, Marketing, Accounting, Advertising, Shipping & Receiving, and Management Strategies.*

You know that somebody may have goofed when writing that, so you start counting the number of seminars named. There are only six! But it says there will be a choice of seven! Which is right? You don't have a rough draft to compare the copy with, so you pick up the phone and call Bill Smith, the person who wrote it. You tell him the problem, and he says, "There are seven, all right—read off the ones you have." You read them to him, and he exclaims: "The typist left out 'Telemarketing Techniques'! Thanks for catching it. Add it in, will you."

You fix the announcement, and feel good because you've helped to make it **COMPLETE**.

To be **CORRECT** you must double-check everything, especially anything with numerals in it, or anything that is a name. If something is stated as a fact, and you don't know whether it's true or not (and, remember, if you don't know, you have to assume that it is not a fact), you must do some research. Check the source. It may be a lot of work, and you may find that it really is a fact, but you have the satisfaction of knowing that what is going to be read by many others is true.

Perhaps nothing irritates a person more than seeing his or her name misspelled. Every name must be checked carefully. And name checking isn't easy either; some names have many different spellings. Take the name "Snyder," for example: it could be *Snyder*, but it could also be *Schneider, Schneiter, Schnieder,* or even *Snider*.

If all else fails, draw a circle around the part you think may be incorrect and put a question mark next to it. That's the "query the author" sign. The person who wrote what you're editing will have to tell you whether it is correct or not. At least, you'll have done your job.

To be **CONSISTENT** is easier, because all the checking is inside the text you are editing.

For example, if what you are reading contains a list of questions, you have to make sure every item in the list is, indeed, a question. Or, if a person is called "Robin A. Morris" in one place, and "Robin H. Morris" in another place, and you know the name refers to the same person, you

91

have to make a change in one of them. And, as a proofreader, you already know about consistency of subjects and verbs. The name of the game is checking, double-checking, back-checking, and rechecking.

To answer that first question that editors ask: **IS IT ACCURATE?** you now know what you must do. You must make certain that what you are editing is COMPLETE, CORRECT, AND CONSISTENT.

LET'S TRY! 6-1

Edit and proofread to eliminate and substitute for inaccuracies of content and spelling.

0. On Wednesday we will be honored with the visitation of ~~four~~ three astronauts: James Bell, Veronica Salazar, and Boris Andrevitch.

1. On Thursday, April 31, Ms. Helga Schneider will address the staff on "Computers in the 21st Century." Ms. Schneizer is the founder of the Macrohard Computer Programs Corporation.

2. The figures tell the story: Our total cost was $4,526 — $2,000 for printing and binding; $2,040 for sales expense; and $536 for incidentals.

3. Did you know:

   a. That newborn kangaroos can fit in a teaspoon?

   b. That the number of people alive on earth now is greater than the number of people who have lived and died on earth up to now?

   c. That Reno, Nevada, is further west than Los Angeles, California?

   d. That time is the fourth dimension?

(Check your work in the Correct Markings *section at the back of this book.)*

(TEMPLATE USERS: Complete this exercise using your template disk.)

Is It Clear?

To be **CLEAR**, a piece of writing *must use words that are familiar* to the people who are going to read it. If the piece is written for scientists, for example, it's okay for it to contain scientific words, like "precipitation" or "optimum," instead of "rain" or "best possible." But if the piece is a weather report to be read by the general public, then it had better say "rain (or snow) tonight," rather than "precipitation likely tonight"; or an annual report should say something like, "Our profits were the best they could be under the circumstances," rather than "We achieved the optimum profit level."

To be **CLEAR**, a piece of writing *must use precise words*. That means it should spell out the date of a meeting, the time it should start, and where it will take place, rather than say something like: "Our annual meeting will take place in two days at the corporate offices." (Two days from when? Where in the corporate offices?) It would be much clearer if it said, "Our annual meeting will take place at 10 a.m. on Friday, January 6, in conference room A at the corporate offices."

To be **CLEAR**, a piece of writing *must use strong, up-to-date words*. For example, a lot of people use similes or metaphors that were very clever and attention-getting when they were first used, but that have now become stale. A letter that begins, "I've been as busy as a bee lately," was probably written by someone who hasn't had a new idea in years. If the writer changes it to "I've been as busy as an ant at a picnic," he is still out of date. Customers may not want to do business with someone who uses phrases like those, rather than words that are new and related to the time we're now living in. If a writer can't think of a new simile, he or she should simply say, "I've been busy lately." The same comment goes for other clichés.

Examples:

(Try restating these to avoid the clichés.)

The company went *belly-up*.

All that counts is *the bottom line*.

What you see is just *the tip of the iceberg*.

If sales don't increase, we'll *throw in the towel*.

Run the idea up a flagpole, and see if anyone salutes.

This campaign will be *the acid test*.

Similar to clichés are old-fashioned, overused, hackneyed expressions. How would you feel if you got a letter reading like this: *"Pursuant to your request of the 12th inst., we hereby tender our reply"*? Isn't this better: *"Here is our answer to the question in your January 12 letter"*? A lot of language dinosaurs are still alive.

Overused Expressions	**Better**
I'd like to thank you for . . .	Thank you for . . .
We want to thank you for . . .	Thank you for . . .
. . . in terms of . . .	by; in relation to; considering
at your earliest convenience	soon
due to the fact that . . .	because
at this point in time	now
the true facts	the facts
In the event that	if

Now that you have an idea of what overused, tired, stale, old-fashioned, hackneyed expressions are like, you know what to look for. Editors especially, but also proofreaders, should get rid of them.

Is it Logical?

To be **LOGICAL,** a piece of writing should have these characteristics:

1. The main idea or purpose of the piece should be clear to the reader.
2. Each paragraph should express one main idea.
3. The idea expressed in the first paragraph should be followed logically by the idea expressed in the next paragraph, and so on through to the end of the piece.
4. At the same time, the ideas expressed in each paragraph should relate logically to the main idea of the whole piece.
5. The ideas expressed in each paragraph should flow smoothly and in logical sequence from one paragraph to the next, either *inductively* or *deductively.*

   INDUCTIVELY means leading toward the main point, with the main point as the conclusion, or culmination.

   DEDUCTIVELY means the main point is stated first, and everything that follows supports it.

LET'S TRY!

6-2

Edit and proofread to eliminate and possibly substitute for clichés, hackneyed expressions, illogicality, and misspellings.

0. I'm busy ~~as a bee~~, so I can't ~~be up to snuff~~ concentrate when I get to your ~~monkey~~ business.

1. ~~Pursuant~~ In answer to your question ~~as to the~~ about accuracy of the jury's decision, ~~at this point in time~~ I think they were right as rain.

2. ~~I would like to express~~ Thank you for my appreciation for ~~your shouldering the burden~~ taking over ~~at the point in time~~ when everyone else ~~had~~ left ~~flown the coop~~.

3. ~~What a cool speech he gave, man!~~ He gave a great speech. It was clear as crystal that he ~~digs~~ understands the importance of ~~the bottom line~~ making a profit ~~in this rat-race of a~~ business.

4. ~~Follow these steps~~ to make a pot of coffee: (1) put two scoops of ground coffee in the basket, (2)(4) put a new filter paper in the basket, (3) ~~pour ten cups of cold water into the pot~~, (4) ~~fill the pot to the ten-cup level~~, (5)(3) pour the cold water that is in the pot into the back of the coffee machine, (6) turn the coffee machine switch to ON, and (7)(3) put the pot under the overhang of the coffee machine.

(Check your work in the Correct Markings *section at the back of this book.)*

(TEMPLATE USERS: Complete this exercise using your template disk.)

Is it Concise?

To be **CONCISE**, a piece of writing *should have no unnecessary words.* Really that means that the piece of writing should be accurate, clear, and logical, and, at the same time, use no more words than are necessary to convey precisely the meaning that the writer intends and that the audience can understand.

English is, by nature, a *redundant* language. That is, it repeats its meanings several times. English is nearly 50 percent redundant. That means that if you read or hear about half of what someone wrote or someone said, you'd be able to get the general idea of what they wrote or said. For example, chances are that if you leave out at random half the letters in a normal sentence, you could complete that sentence the way it was originally written. Let's try it: What does this say? I _ _ G O _ _ G T _ _ H E M _ V _ _ S.

Did you decide it said, "I am going to the movies"? This is why we enjoy games like "hangman," "Wheel of Fortune," "Scrabble," crossword puzzles, and the simple cryptography features in the newspaper. We can read what isn't there because we know some of it. This redundancy of meaning is probably what makes the English language the most widely used language on earth. But we don't have to make it more redundant than it is.

For example, why should we say "at the present time," when we have a perfectly good, short, single word that means the same thing—NOW? Why should we write "consensus of opinion," when the word "consensus," itself, means "an opinion held together by a group"? Why should we write "during the time that," when we have that perfectly good word: WHILE—or just DURING? Why say "end result," when results always occur at the end, anyway, and just plain RESULT is enough?

Name some shorter, or more accurate, forms of the following:

Basic fundamentals	*basics or fundamentals*
Continue on	*continue or go on*
We are in agreement	*we agree*
In the near future	*soon*
Past history	*past or history*
Personal opinion	*opinion*
True facts	*facts*
Come to the conclusion	*decide*

Another thing—introductory words take up a lot of space and don't really mean much. In phrases such as "There is," "There are," or "It is," for example, what does *There* mean? What does *It* mean? How much stronger a sentence is if it says: *I believe him*, instead of *It is my belief that he is correct*.

That sentence, "I believe him," is a good, clear, concise sentence. But if you have a longer sentence and throw in "I believes" or "in my opinions" or phrases like that, you are usually wasting space. The person who is writing surely *believes* what he or she is writing, doesn't he or she?

TO BE CONCISE, TAKE ALL THIS ADVICE.

Class Exercise 6-1

Directions: Edit the following letter so that it is clear and concise.

November 17, 19--

Mrs. A. W. Schaefer
24 Kingston St.
Corinth, NY 12822

Dear Mrs. Schaeffer:

Our records ~~at this point in time~~ show that you have not used your Willard's charge card ~~for purchases at our store~~ for ~~a period of~~ over six months. ~~Due to the fact that~~ Because you have been a valued customer of Willard's since 1972, ~~it is our desire in this written communication to express our gratitude~~ we want to thank you for your previous patronage ~~in the past~~ and ~~to tender an~~ invitation ~~to~~ you to ~~pay a~~ visit ~~to~~ Willard's during ~~a special~~ all-day sale ~~to be held~~ a week from next Saturday. ~~If you will just keep~~ this letter ~~and~~ bring ~~it~~ with you to the sale and give it to the sales clerk when you make your first purchase, you will receive 20% off that purchase.

In addition, ~~extending~~ throughout the ~~duration of the~~ sale Willard's will offer to ~~each and~~ every shopper ~~the provision of~~ free ~~complimentary~~ gift wrapping ~~without charge~~ for any item over ~~and above~~ $25 ~~in cost~~ purchased on the day of the sale.

We ~~look forward~~ hope to be ~~ing~~ of service to you again as we have ~~been~~ in the past.

Sincerely,

Linda Piperson
Credit Manager

(TEMPLATE USERS: Complete this exercise using your template disk.)

JOB READY?   You should be ready to do Job Sheets 28* and 29* now!

Avoid the Passive Voice

Good writing should be in the active voice, not the passive voice. Whatever a company or an individual writes is supposed to DO something for the company or for that individual. It is not supposed to just sit there, doing nothing, waiting for something to happen.

Some examples will show the difference:

PASSIVE VOICE: *The man was bitten by the dog.*

This is a perfectly good sentence grammatically. It has a subject (*man*), a verb (*was bitten*), and a prepositional phrase with the word *dog* as its object related to the verb. But who performed the action of the verb; who did the biting? The dog! Biting is a pretty strong action, and yet the one who performed the action is relegated to the passive position in this sentence of being merely an object — not even a direct object, but the object of a preposition! And the subject (*man*) just sits passively by and receives the bite. The sentence doesn't DO anything; it just tells tamely something that happened. Let's put it in the active voice.

ACTIVE VOICE: *The dog bit the man.*

Now the one (*the dog*) that performed the action, the DOer, is the subject of the sentence. That makes sense. The one (*the man*) who received the action is the direct object of the action. That makes sense, too. The sentence is short, clear, and to the point. It ACTS. If virtually all sentences, no matter how long or involved, follow this pattern — that is, if the performer of the action (or the initiator of the state of being) described by the verb is the subject, and if the receiver of the action (or the beneficiary of the state of being) described by the verb is the direct object — the sentence will be strong, active, and good.

A good editor looks for weak, passive sentences in whatever he or she edits and changes them to strong, active sentences.

> **LET'S TRY!** 6-3

Edit and proofread to eliminate and substitute for wordiness, redundancy, and unnecessary use of the passive voice.

0. ~~It's my personal opinion that it~~ *I think* ha~~s~~ve too often ~~been~~ alleged ~~by the media~~ that bureaucrats are lazy~~, and don't work.~~ The ~~true~~ facts are, and ~~past~~ history has shown, that most bureaucrats ~~work hard and~~ are very industrious.

   If ~~only~~ the leaders of nations were ~~all~~ aware of the ~~basic~~ fundamentals of freedom and liberty, there could be no war ~~nor armed conflict~~. They would be forced ~~by those same basic fundamentals~~ to ~~come to the~~ realize ~~conclusion~~ that war is not the solution ~~to the problematical question as~~ to how people should live together~~, side by side~~. They would know that war is useless~~, of no utility, and lacking in any value~~. At ~~the present~~ Right now time, our greatest need ~~and necessity~~ is to enable these leaders to ~~learn and~~ increase their awareness.

(Check your work in the Correct Markings section at the back of this book.)

💾 **(TEMPLATE USERS:** Complete this exercise using your template disk.)

JOB READY? You should be ready to do Job Sheet 30* now!

Class Exercise 6-2

Directions: Following a class discussion of the content of this Exercise, rewrite the sentences below, which are written in the passive voice, so that they are in the active voice.

1. It was announced today by Madelyn Kofsky, Acme's Human Resources Director, that Frank D'Angelo will be succeeded as head of the Parts Department by Robert Gladwin.

    REWRITE: *Acme's Human Resources Director, MK, announced that RG will succeed FD'A as head of the PD.*

2. It was remarked by Mr. Gladwin that he has a tough act to follow.

    REWRITE: *Mr. Gladwin remarked that he has a tough act to follow.*

3. Mr. D'Angelo's career started 30 years ago when he was asked by Acme's founder to join the firm.

    REWRITE: *Acme's founder asked Mr. D'Angelo to join the firm, and that's what started his career 30 years ago when —*

4. Mr. D'Angelo is an avid golfer, so it is predicted by his friends that he'll enjoy his retirement.

    REWRITE: *Mr. D'Angelo's friends predict that he'll enjoy his retirement, because he is an avid golfer.*

5. A reception in his honor is being planned by his co-workers.

    REWRITE: *His co-workers are planning a reception in his honor.*

Notice that most passive-voice sentences contain the word "by" — something was done to somebody by something or somebody. Also notice that the verb form in a passive-voice sentence usually contains a helping verb, such as "is" or "was" — something "was done" ... "by." Look for "bys" and helping verbs, and you'll find passive-voice sentences more easily. Once you find them, make them active.

(TEMPLATE USERS: Complete this exercise using your template disk.)

Wrap-Up

Editors ask whether a piece of writing is **accurate**. That means is it **complete, correct, and consistent?** They ask whether a piece of writing is **clear**. That means are the words **familiar, precise, strong, and up to date?** They ask whether a piece of writing is **logical**. That means does it **flow, have a main idea, interrelate?** And they ask whether a piece of writing is **concise;** i.e., does it contain **no unnecessary words?**

Correct Markings for the "Let's Try" Exercises

Correct Markings for the "Let's Try" Exercises

LET'S TRY 1-1 (p. 4)
1. The ~~the~~ goal of business is to make a profit.
2. Successful business people know that they can make more profit in the long run if they sell a quality product and if they have good public relations.
3. A customer [insert apostrophe]'s goodwill depends upon how much and what kind of service he or she gets.
4. Goodwill also depends upon whether business executives appear to have the [insert quotation marks] You Attitude [insert comma]," rather than to be thinking of themselves or their business all the time.
5. So it is correct to say that in business one can do well by doing good.

LET'S TRY 1-2 (p. 5)
1. There are at least seven days in a work week.
2. The best qualification you have/can to get a job is dependability.
3. What should I say? "He could count on one only friend," or "He only could count on one friend."
4. I can listen to you the/for moment, but not for all day.
5. The way to write one thousand in numerals is 10,00.

LET'S TRY 1-3 (p. 7)
FORMATTING A REPORT

There are probably dozens of correct ways to format a short written report, but the way I learned works well for me. First, I center the main heading at the top of the page, using all capital letters. Then I leave a space blank and start the text. It's pretty standard, I think, to start each

new paragraph indented five spaces from the left margin. After that, of course, all the lines go back to the left margin until the end of the paragraph.

If you're using a subheading within the report, you should set it off in some way, probably by putting it on a line by itself. I usually underline it or, if I can, use italic or boldface type.

102

LET'S TRY 1-4 (p. 9)

It's no fun working with oldfashioned computers. Allcomputers can not be the most current, ofcourse. Still, it would be good if all offices and all schools couldhave the pleasure of having state-of-the-art computers. [Mark a new paragraph here] Ironically, it is the computer industry itself that keeps us from getting truly state-of-the-art computers. You see, they come up with new ideas so fast that, by the time we get the latest thing they develop, they have already developed something else that is truly more powerful, and what we have is no longer state-of-the-art equipment. [Do not begin a new paragraph here] It isn'tfair, isit?

LET'S TRY 1-5 (p. 10)

1. Sometimes even proofreaders make mistakes, and if a sec'y happens to catch a proofreader's mistake, he or she should become a super proofreader and mark it "stet."
2. The principal officers of the company are Natalie Jones, Chair of the Board; Juan Gonzales, CEO; Yashima Ogata, Pres; and Lu Wong, Treasurer.
3. A person should always count ~~his or her~~ their change before leaving the cash reg.

LET'S TRY 1-6 (p. 12)

Some people think that to emphasize words or phrases it is appropriate to use boldface type, which you show in this way: Spring is here! or Spring is here! But others disagree. They think you should use italics, which you show in this way: Spring is here! or Spring is here! Still others think you should emphasize by using all capitals, which you show in this way: Spring is here! or Spring is here! Nobody, though, would show emphasis by making a capitalized word or phrase all lowercase, but if they wanted to change all caps to all lowercase for some other reason, they would show it in this way: SPRING IS HERE! or SPRING IS HERE! And if they wanted to make it caps and lowercase as it would appear in a title, they would show it this way: spring is here and everywhere!

103

LET'S TRY 1-7 (p. 15)

Reading proof [insert left parenthesis] i.e., the "proof" that what was meant to be typed on a keyboard actually was typed and printed out [insert right parenthesis] demands concentration [insert dash] not relaxation and enjoyment and [insert ellipsis] well, you know what I mean.

Proofreading is finding and correcting errors.[insert asterisk]Concentration is required because (even though the original copy may be very neat [and neatness is important[insert right bracket]] [insert right parenthesis] an error could possibly appear with each character you look at.

A good proofreader seems to enjoy the concentration [insert dash] even when he or she proofreads his or her own writings [insert left parenthesis] that is, when he or she is a combination writer [insert slash] proofreader).

_____
*An error is a faulty use or non-use of the proper forms of words and sentences, misuse of punctuation, or misspelling.

LET'S TRY 1-8 (p. 18)

He received the reciept and felt that he acheived the goal he had always beleived in. Happily, he put the receipt in his breifcase and began walking to the feista where he was supposed to meet his neice. No longer would she greive over the loss of her office and her place in the heirarchy of the club. Now she would be releived, not of her position as cheif, but in her heart. She would get a repreive. And he could take a seista while he waited for her to arrive.

104

Let's Try 2-1 (p. 23)

noun 1. What is the name of (or word used for) a person, place, thing, or idea?
subject 2. What is a word that performs the action that an action-verb describes?
verb 3. What links subjects with objects or descriptions of subjects?
pronoun 4. What is a word that substitutes for a noun?
object 5. What is a word that receives the action described by an action-verb?
verb 6. What is a word (or group of words) that tells the action a subject is performing?
verb 7. What is a word (or group of words) that tells the state of being of a subject, or links a subject to another part of a sentence?
clause 8. What is a group of words that has both a subject and verb, and acts either independently in a sentence (as a sentence within a sentence), or is dependent upon the rest of the sentence to complete the thought of a sentence?

Let's Try 2-2 (p. 29)

1. Every one of the plates ~~are~~ *is* chipped or cracked.
2. Two dollars ~~are~~ *is* a lot to pay for an ice cream bar, but Dream bars are worth it.
3. The fine for overdue books ~~are~~ *is* five cents a day.
4. A few miles beyond the intersection of Bridge and Thompson ~~are~~ *is* a bunch of fast-food restaurants.
5. Neither Dad nor his brothers ~~was~~ *were* able to go to college.
6. The results of a questionnaire circulated throughout the department indicate~~s~~ that some of the staff wishe~~s~~ they could skip the company picnic and just have the day off instead.
7. She said most of the sentences in my report to the Grievance Committee need~~s~~ to be shortened.
8. Anybody with that many charge cards ~~are~~ *is* just asking for trouble.
9. Bill or Jake ~~have~~ *has* offered to drive us home after the meeting.
10. The memo said the canned goods ~~is~~ *are* to be taken to the loading dock before the end of the workday on Friday.
11. I heard that Jean and maybe Paula, too, ~~has~~ *have* signed up for the course.
12. Before all the publicity about the dangers of salt and cholesterol, ham and eggs ~~were~~ *was* famous as an all-American dish.
13. The media ~~is~~ *are* having a field day with the rumors all his former colleagues at the agency ~~is~~ *are* spreading about him.
14. The number of responses we received to the special mailing ~~were~~ *was* disappointing, to say the least.
15. Whether to take more courses in English or in economics ~~are~~ *is* something I have to decide.

105

LET'S TRY 2-3 (p. 34)

1. Between you and ~~I~~ *me*, the manager is proud of ~~she~~ *her* and ~~I~~ *me*.
2. I don't know who*m* is going to the convention.
3. The doctor gave h~~e~~ *im* a clean bill of health.
4. To ~~who~~ *Whom* It May Concern:
5. The argument was between him and ~~she~~ *her*.

LET'S TRY 2-4 (p. 36)

1. He was absolut*e*ly aw*e*some when he played his guitar.
2. "I was only jok~~e~~ing," said Julio, typ~~e~~ing his memoirs.
3. The chef was bak~~e~~ing in the bak*e*ry, wiggl~~e~~ing his fingers.
4. He let out a pierc~~e~~ing scream. It was very notic*e*able.
5. Chen Li's greatest achiev*e*ment was mak~~e~~ing money.

LET'S TRY 3-1 (p. 44)

1. Yes, I think we should go to the concert.
2. Curly, the clown, is the funniest person I ever saw.
3. The boss' secretary, however, wouldn't let the applicant enter the door.
4. The automobile, which had just had a brake job, could stop on a dime.
5. Would you please make 25 copies of this, Melissa?
6. Yes, the colorful float, which took a year to decorate, won the prize.
7. Tom, Dick, and Harry all like to ride, hunt, and fish.
8. The automobile that is quiet, that gives good gasoline mileage, that has enough power to climb hills, that has a good warranty, and that has dual airbags is the one to buy.
9. She also plays the drums rhythmically, expertly, and loudly.
10. I went to the mall, and I bought a shirt.
11. I went to the mall and bought a shirt.
12. Successful retail stores say their attitude is that their customers come first.
13. "I'm ready to go," said Ashley.
14. The article in *Golf Tips*, the magazine, was entitled, "How To Swing."

106

LET'S TRY 3-2 (p. 48)

1. Buy the workbook**;** borrow the textbook.
2. Kieran was a very serious person**;** accordingly, he never laughed at jokes.
3. Maria inadvertently missed the bus**,** but she got a ride with Jeanne.
4. Maria inadvertently missed the bus**;** still**,** she got a ride.
5. The party lost faith in their candidate**;** they decided to vote for someone else.
6. Pete, the plumber**;** Elena, the electrician**;** Carlos, the carpenter**;** and Paola, the plasterer**,** formed a company to build inexpensive houses.
7. Let's see America! First, Boston, Massachusetts**;** then New York City**;** then Washington, DC**;** then Detroit, Michigan**;** then Chicago, Illinois; then Santa Fe, New Mexico**;** then San Francisco, California**;** then Tucson, Arizona**;** then New Orleans, Louisiana**;** and end up in Miami, Florida.

LET'S TRY 3-3 (p. 51)

It's high time I convey**e**d my thanks to you for the beaut**i**ful party. I had to leave earl**i**er than I wanted to because of pressing bus**i**ness dut**ie**s (a meeting with some lobbyists and their attorn**ey**s), but not before I'd **paid** (~~payed~~) a visit to the bount**i**ful buffet table; admired the artistic bouquets of dais**ie**s, baby's breath, peon**ie**s, and lil**ie**s of the valley; and happ**i**ly sampled the elegant grocer**ie**s **laid** (~~layed~~) out there. When I described the spread to Margaret—roast beef, lobster rolls, cand**i**ed apples, and not just one but two smoked turk**ey**s—she **said** (~~sayed~~), "Everybody knows that your abilit**ie**s at giving part**ie**s are unmatched."

Let's Try 3-4 (p. 52)

The rivalr*ies* that crop up among chemists who do chemical analys*es* really have no solid bas*es*. And they aren't really battles between the sex*es*, even though the numbers of m*en* and wom*en* among such chemists are about equal. Instead, the frequent cris*es* occur simply because the criteri*a* for analysis differ so much among them. And each chemist, of course, thinks he or she is correct — so correct, in fact, that you would think they all had halo*es* around their heads. Still, their dat*a* are different, and their medi*a* of communication are mixed. To evaluate them truly, one must study carefully the appendi*c*es of their many books.

Let's Try 4-1 (p. 57)

1. At 7 p.m. I am going to leave for the concert.
2. The card measured 3 in. by 5 in. so that it would slip in easily.
3. The comedian asked why they didn't laugh at his jokes.
4. The comedian asked, "Why don't you laugh at my jokes?"
5. Yes! (or Yes.) The profits last year were fantastic! (or .)
6. Would you please send your payment immediately.
7. You went off to Chicago without telling me. Why?
8. John's IQ was 140, but he got only a "C."
9. HI is the two-letter designation for Hawaii.

Let's Try 4-2 (p. 62)

1. I promise to pay the sum of fourteen dollars and twelve cents ($14.12) on or before March 15, 1995.
2. The rules of the game (I found them in the attic) are to be followed precisely.
3. I think—no, I know—we should acquire that company.
4. There's only one thing to do — accept their terms.
5. When they walked off the plane (what a dishevelled group they were — wrinkled and drooping with fatigue) Sebastian popped open a bottle of champagne [imported] for them.

Let's Try 4-3 (p.64)

1. When you use closed punctuation in a business letter, your salutation should read, "Dear _____:" and "Sincerely yours," is the way your complimentary close should read.
2. There four steps in writing a sales letter: (1) gain attention, (2) create interest, (3) develop desire, and (4) get action.
3. My grandmother's favorite Bible passage was Matthew 10:5.
4. I'll meet you at 2:15 this afternoon.
5. This would be Vol. II:10 of the newsletter.

Let's Try 4-4 (p.67)

The administrative assistant was barring the door when Wolfgang tried to gain admittance to the director's office. "Stop begging me to get in," she said. "None of your clever maneuvering will do any good. You certainly won't be eliciting any positive responses from me!" Wolfgang, however, was merely fulfilling his promise to the director not to leave without visiting him once more. Wolfgang was beginning to get angry. He could see that yelling would do no good; there were obviously grave differences in their interpretations of the situation. So he decided to be personable. He smiled charmingly and said, "Look, I wasn't kidding; he really wants to see me. You could be buzzing him to find out. Would you do that?" Still glowering, she picked up the phone. She learned that Wolfgang was right. Reluctantly, she decided that letting him in was the thing to do. She had no rebuttal.

Let's Try 5-1 (p.71)

1. The women's movement has brought about many changes.
2. The pickup truck's headlights were set too high.
3. Phyliss's husband was a telemarketing supervisor.
4. There was no place to check the ladies' purses.
5. Food was better at the enlisted men's and women's mess than at the officers' mess.
6. Everyone's car should be checked for emissions.
7. The stray cat is not Mary's, Gus's, Jill's, or anyone else's.

109

Let's Try 5-2 (p. 72)

1. Did(n't) he tell you I'm going to be here?
2. We're happy to be out of the '60s era.
3. They've been at 6's and 7's all their lives. They're always at cross purposes.
4. You're going to get your comeuppance someday.
5. George said to arrive by six o'clock.

Let's Try 5-3 (p. 73)

1. ~~Its / it's~~ own trademark. *or It's its own trademark.*
2. I don't know who's going, nor whose car this is.
3. These groceries are ours, those are yours, and those others are ~~they'res~~. *theirs*.
4. It's not going to be easy.
5. Where did it get its name?

Let's Try 5-4 (p. 75)

1. The tennis coach said that "Arturo is sure to win the match."
2. The tennis coach's actual words were, "Arturo is sure to win the match."
3. She said, "I hope you have a nice trip," and then she cried.
4. The word "tía" is Spanish for aunt.
5. He tried to recall his actual thoughts. Yes, they were "Why did I put down my briefcase before knocking on the door?"
6. The only program he watched on CBS was "60 Minutes."

Let's Try 5-5 (p. 77)

When my grandfather was in his eighties, he came to live with Dad and Mom and me. He was fun to talk to, and I spent a lot of time with him.

"Gramp," I said one day, "tell me about your first job after college."

"Well, I felt pretty lucky to get a job," he said. "Jobs were hard to find in those days, and when they said, 'You're hired—report for work Monday morning at eight,' I couldn't believe my ears.

"I felt like a big shot reporting for work in the brand-new suit the folks had bought me when I graduated. When the supervisor saw me, his jaw dropped. 'What's that getup you're wearing?' he asked. 'You'll wear overalls like everybody else on the shop floor.'

"Remember, Todd, I had my engineering degree by then. But I learned in a hurry that an engineer just starting out had to show that he knew how to clean and fix a machine before he'd be given a job designing one. It wasn't what I hoped to spend my whole life doing, but I'd grown up hearing my parents say, 'All work is noble.' It drove me crazy to hear that quoted over and over again when I was a kid, and I groused about having to spend Saturday morning cleaning the garage or polishing the car, but it's been pretty helpful at times."

Let's Try 5-6 (p. 79)

1. The word "molybdenum"* is difficult to pronounce.
2. As a young lad he lived on a farm where his life consisted mostly of hiking, climbing trees, and taking care of animals.

    Twenty years later, he was still hiking, climbing trees, and taking care of animals. He worked in a zoo.
3. "Mary had a little lamb. And everywhere that Mary went, the lamb was sure to go."

---

*"Molybdenum" is a metallic element used chiefly to make a hard steel alloy.

111

Let's Try 5-7 (p. 84)

1. Although he seemed self-assured, he was really filled with self-doubt.
2. Although almost three-quarters of the earth is covered with water, 100 percent of the people on earth live on the land.
3. The new edition of the book has been brought completely up-to-date.
4. The up-to-date edition of the book is just off the presses.
5. All told, the all-time all-Americans are few.
6. She gave them the go-ahead, but they gave her the run-around.
7. His great-aunt was really great.
8. One thing about her was that she was full of self-determination.
9. My mother-in-law became president-elect of the club.

Let's Try 5-8 (p. 88)

It takes good management to spell every word correctly, but when a company does so, it finds the practice very advantageous, because it shows that the company is knowledgeable. There's a horseshoeing business out West that misspells words all the time, and instead of being courageous enough to hire someone to teach their horseshoers how to spell, the owners misspend their money on illicit, illogical, and irrational projects. It's really outrageous what they do. They are truly irresponsible.

Let's Try 6-1 (p. 92)

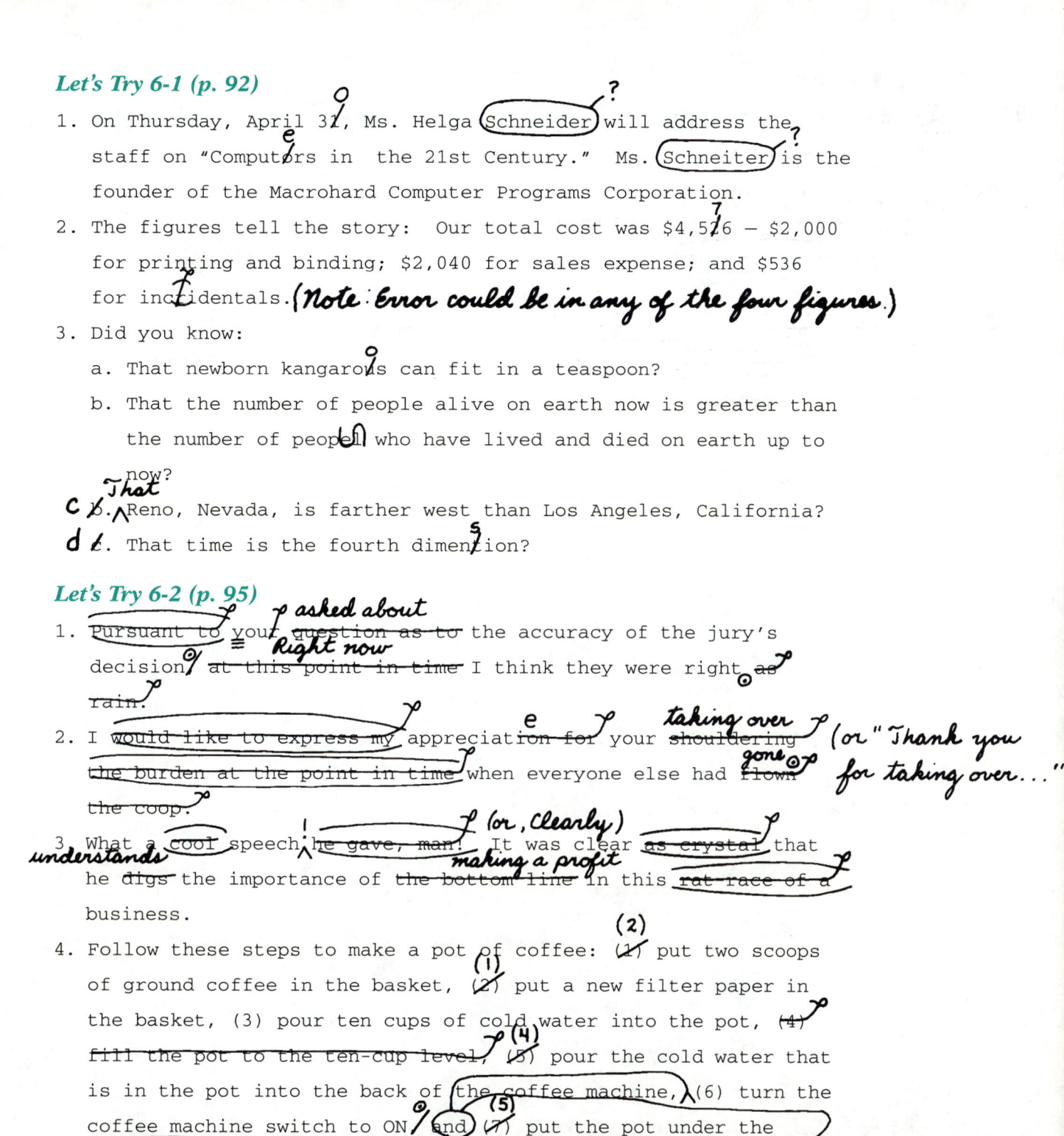

1. On Thursday, April 31, Ms. Helga Schneider will address the staff on "Computers in the 21st Century." Ms. Schneiter is the founder of the Macrohard Computer Programs Corporation. [marks: 31→o?, Computers→e, Schneider circled ?, Schneiter circled ?] (Note: Error could be in any of the four figures.)

2. The figures tell the story: Our total cost was $4,576 − $2,000 for printing and binding; $2,040 for sales expense; and $536 for incidentals.

3. Did you know:
   a. That newborn kangaroos can fit in a teaspoon?
   b. That the number of people alive on earth now is greater than the number of people who have lived and died on earth up to now?
   c. That Reno, Nevada, is farther west than Los Angeles, California?
   d. That time is the fourth dimension?

Let's Try 6-2 (p. 95)

1. ~~Pursuant to your question as to~~ [asked about] the accuracy of the jury's decision, ~~at this point in time~~ [Right now] I think they were right ~~as rain~~.

2. I ~~would like to express my~~ appreciation ~~for~~ your ~~shouldering the burden at the point in time~~ [taking over] when everyone else had ~~flown the coop~~ [gone]. (or "Thank you for taking over...")

3. What a ~~cool~~ speech ~~he gave, man!~~ It was clear ~~as crystal~~ (or, Clearly) that he ~~digs~~ [understands] the importance of ~~the bottom line~~ [making a profit] in this ~~rat-race of a~~ business.

4. Follow these steps to make a pot of coffee: (1) put two scoops of ground coffee in the basket, (2) put a new filter paper in the basket, (3) pour ten cups of cold water into the pot, ~~(4) fill the pot to the ten-cup level,~~ (4)[was 5] pour the cold water that is in the pot into the back of the coffee machine, (6) turn the coffee machine switch to ON, and (5) put the pot under the overhang of the coffee machine. (Rewrite into the revised sequence)

Let's Try 6-3 (p. 99)

¶ If ~~only~~ the leaders of nations were ~~all~~ aware of the ~~basic~~ fundamentals of freedom and liberty, there could be no war~~, nor armed conflict~~. They would be forced ~~by those same basic fundamentals~~ to ~~come to the conclusion~~ *conclude* that war is not the solution to the ~~problematical~~ question as to how people should live together~~, side by side~~. They would know that war is useless~~, of no utility, and lacking in any value~~. ~~At the present time~~ *Now*, our greatest need ~~and necessity~~ is to enable these leaders to ~~learn and~~ increase their awareness.

Official State Abbreviations

Here are the official United States Postal Service abbreviations for all the 50 states, plus the District of Columbia:

AL	Alabama	**MT**	Montana
AK	Alaska	**NE**	Nebraska
AZ	Arizona	**NV**	Nevada
AR	Arkansas	**NH**	New Hampshire
CA	California	**NJ**	New Jersey
CO	Colorado	**NM**	New Mexico
CT	Connecticut	**NY**	New York
DE	Delaware	**NC**	North Carolina
DC	District of Columbia	**ND**	North Dakota
FL	Florida	**OH**	Ohio
GA	Georgia	**OK**	Oklahoma
HI	Hawaii	**OR**	Oregon
ID	Idaho	**PA**	Pennsylvania
IL	Illinois	**RI**	Rhode Island
IN	Indiana	**SC**	South Carolina
IA	Iowa	**SD**	South Dakota
KS	Kansas	**TN**	Tennessee
KY	Kentucky	**TX**	Texas
LA	Louisiana	**UT**	Utah
ME	Maine	**VT**	Vermont
MD	Maryland	**VA**	Virginia
MA	Massachusetts	**WA**	Washington
MI	Michigan	**WV**	West Virginia
MN	Minnesota	**WI**	Wisconsin
MS	Mississippi	**WY**	Wyoming
MO	Missouri		